I ♥ KOSHER

BEAUTIFUL RECIPES FROM MY KITCHEN

KIM KUSHNER

To Milan, Emanuel, Rafaela & Jude ♥

photography
KATE SEARS

weldon**owen**

CONTENTS

INTRODUCTION

Writing a cookbook is one thing. Writing an introduction to a cookbook—my cookbook—is a whole other thing. For me, the recipes are the easy part (just ask my editor, Amy!). Ideas and flavor combinations flow in and out of my brain nonstop, and I love testing and perfecting recipes. It's so fun sharing my latest concoctions on social media and getting responses from so many of you! I love the "creating" part of the creative process, from coming up with a concept and researching recipes and ingredients through travel to experiencing different flavors in restaurants and reading books and asking lots of questions. I love meeting new people and learning about their culture through food. My husband teases me because he knows I always ask two questions when I meet someone new while traveling abroad: Where are you from? What do you eat there?

That's why I have always loved cookbooks. I have a large collection of cookbooks, and before buying a new one, I read the introduction first. The introduction serves as my first peek into the author's soul. More often than not, if I like the author's style in their introduction, I will like the book (hope you're liking this so far!). This is why a cookbook introduction is so daunting. My favorite cookbooks aren't necessarily the ones I cook from most. I can fall in love with a cookbook because of its author, its beautiful images, or perhaps because of its vibe, but often, the cookbooks I use the most are the ones with the fewest photographs, the simplest ingredients, and the shortest instructions. I guess that's a reflection of my cooking style, where less is more. I don't like much fuss in the kitchen, and I aim to create recipes that are simple enough to memorize. I like a clean page, just a few ingredients on the list, and straightforward directions. I enjoy food that tastes like what it started out as. I'm drawn to color, texture, and bold, fresh flavors.

This is the third cookbook I have authored. My objective, much like my recipes, is simple: it's to give you an entire book that offers go-to, tried-and-true recipes that you can rely on for any and every occasion and for any meal of the day. The recipes I've included guarantee stellar results for meals you don't want to take any chances on and for when you need something that's going to be a major crowd-pleaser but can be executed with simplicity. Here you can find those time-tested recipes that always deliver. I've thought long and hard about what works in my own kitchen and in my everyday life as a busy mom to four kids, and I've talked to thousands of women and men in the course of promoting my books and doing cooking demonstrations. What I've concluded is that we're all looking for ways to maximize cooking that nourishes on every level. We want fresh, flavor-packed recipes that inspire creativity while adhering to a streamlined set of techniques and ingredients—just the style of cooking I've become known for.

But, it's not only about the recipes—they're just half the battle. It's also about organization. Let me tell you what works for me: being prepared. Having ingredients ready to go. In between taking my baby to the park, meeting my girlfriends for coffee, spending hours on the phone with my sisters (repeating the same conversations we've had daily for 15 years, might I add), and returning whatever it was I bought yesterday, I always find time to cook dinner for my family. Yes, I cook almost every night—it's true. But here's how I do it: I follow a formula I've mastered to use my time and resources smartly, creatively, and simply, yet also in a way that satisfies the sensual needs of my appetite for flavor, aesthetics, fun, and nourishment. And guess what? You can do it too! You can entertain, feed family and friends, or have an intimate everyday meal with style and stimulation . . . without going nuts. Trust me, I spend the better part of most days cooking, be it for my family, for work, or for entertaining and holidays. And in the process of preparing an endless amount

of meals—and writing two well-received cookbooks—I've collected a treasure trove of just these kinds of go-to dishes. I've been fortunate enough to make a career out of offering simple, straightforward recipes that rely on a well-curated collection of easy-to-find ingredients and focus as much on ease as on excellence, and now I want to share them all with you.

And so, I present an entire cookbook full of my dependable standbys, my staples, the kitchen essentials that never disappoint and deliver gorgeous, delicious food you'll be as excited to eat as your family and friends will be. Oh, and they just happen to be kosher too.

The first chapter features what I call my "ready to go" recipes. These are recipes and prepared ingredients to always have on hand; they make throwing together a meal as easy as 1-2-3. Consider the recipes in this chapter your essentials—along with my must-have fridge, freezer, pantry, and equipment lists, illustrated on pages 12–13—if you have a few of these foods stored in your fridge or freezer, on any given day you'll be able to create sophisticated, delicious meals quickly and efficiently. I also include recipes that are so multifunctional that they are a new category of their own: I give you "sip." Yes, "sip"—the word I invented for sauce and dip, or foods that can be used interchangeably as sauces or dips. Easy marinades, quick salad dressings, perfect pickles—you'll find them all tucked away in Chapter 1.

But wait, there's more. Visit Chapter 2 for easy appetizer, snack, and nibbles recipes. These are effortless recipes that are perfect for casual munching. And, everyone loves a gorgeous board; in this chapter I'll show you how to build one. The remaining chapters include recipes for brunch, which is my favorite meal of the day, and for quick stove-top mains (yes, that means main dishes in under an hour!). Or, for one of those lazy days when you're seeking an all-in-one meal, check out the chapter for one-pan meals—you will come back for more. If you have the time, you'll also want to skim the chapter for hearty soups, stews, and fall-off-the-bone mains. For colorful, fresh veggies and sides, flip through the salads and sides chapter. And last, but not least, make your way to the desserts chapter for my sweet delights.

So now, on to the title. I ❤ Kosher—what does it mean? Those of you who know me know that I love to love. What you see is what you get. I'm an all-or-nothing type of person. I love my family and I love my friends. I love life, I love food, and I love to eat, but more than anything else, I love to feed the people around me. What really makes me happy? Good food. Good, kosher food.

When my first cookbook, *The Modern Menu*, was published in 2013, I wanted to demonstrate that a beautiful, modern cookbook could also be a kosher one. By using sleek, gorgeous photography (I also happen to love photographer Andrew Zuckerman), I set out to create a kosher cookbook that was visually unlike any other kosher cookbook. With my second book, *The New Kosher,* I wanted to redefine what kosher meant. It was an exciting time in the kosher world, as so many new voices and points of view were emerging and taking advantage of seasonal, organic ingredients and a farm-to-table style of cooking kosher. I felt empowered being part of this important movement. I've always kept kosher and never thought that this fact should compromise what I cook. I felt that the world around me was finally catching on to the same notion! Kosher food isn't just bagels and lox or matzo ball soup. Kosher food can be fresh, seasonal, colorful, organic, and believe it or not, even healthy. And since *The New Kosher* was published, many wonderful, modern kosher cookbooks have emerged, which only allows this "new kosher" philosophy to flourish further.

Now I find myself in a new position. The world has recognized the turn kosher has taken. Kosher has caught up with the times, and it's time to enjoy its updated philosophy. With this book, I've opened up my home to you, just as you've opened your homes to me. It was a dream of mine to create a book out of my own kitchen, the same kitchen where I cook for my family. This is my way of saying "thank you" to you for following me on my kosher journey. I hope you enjoy the book.

With ❤,
Kim

MY KITCHEN TOOL ESSENTIALS

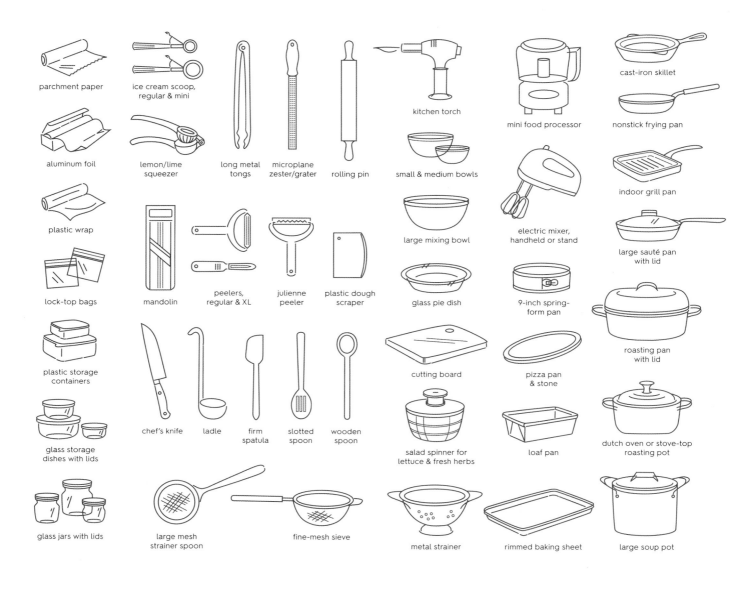

parchment paper

ice cream scoop,
regular & mini

kitchen torch

mini food processor

cast-iron skillet

aluminum foil

lemon/lime
squeezer

long metal
tongs

microplane
zester/grater

rolling pin

small & medium bowls

nonstick frying pan

plastic wrap

large mixing bowl

electric mixer,
handheld or stand

indoor grill pan

lock-top bags

mandolin

peelers,
regular & XL

julienne
peeler

plastic dough
scraper

glass pie dish

9-inch spring-
form pan

large sauté pan
with lid

plastic storage
containers

cutting board

pizza pan
& stone

roasting pan
with lid

glass storage
dishes with lids

chef's knife

ladle

firm
spatula

slotted
spoon

wooden
spoon

salad spinner for
lettuce & fresh herbs

loaf pan

dutch oven or stove-top
roasting pot

glass jars with lids

large mesh
strainer spoon

fine-mesh sieve

metal strainer

rimmed baking sheet

large soup pot

MY PANTRY MUST-HAVES

kosher salt	powdered sugar	white rice	maple syrup	balsamic vinegar	almond butter
sea salt	dark brown sugar	brown rice	pomegranate syrup	light olive oil	nutella
table salt	light brown sugar	couscous	honey	extra-virgin olive oil	tomato sauce
black-pepper mill	shredded coconut	pasta (penne, spaghetti)	silan (date syrup)	canola oil	tomato paste
flour	almond flour	udon noodles	soy sauce	spray oil	sun-dried tomatoes in oil
sugar	bread crumbs	rolled oats	tamari	coconut oil	israeli tea biscuits
baking powder	panko	cocoa powder	white vinegar	roasted sesame oil	instant pudding mix
baking soda	seeds (sunflower,	pure vanilla extract	rice vinegar	tahini	cans of chickpeas
yeast	pumpkin, sesame)	vanilla bean pods	red wine vinegar	peanut butter	cans of white beans

MY FREEZER & FRIDGE ESSENTIALS

dried cherries, cranberries, raisins & medjool dates

shelled edamame

peas

homemade pestos

kataif

chocolate chips

puff pastry

espresso powder

walnuts, almonds, pecans & coconut stored in original packaging or lock-top bags

caramelized onions

chopped spinach

homemade broth

* chicken bones

milk

eggs

orange juice

parmesan block

butter

yogurt, greek & vanilla

low-fat mayonnaise

dark chocolate bars

apricot jam

dijon mustard, grainy & smooth

ketchup

yellow mustard

worcestershire sauce

white miso

tabasco sauce

chocolate syrup

chopped garlic

limes

chopped ginger

lemons

chopped prepped herbs

sliced smoked salmon

apples

oranges

celery

jalapeños

carrots

* potatoes

shredded cabbage

whole onions

SPICE SHELF MUST-HAVES

ground cinnamon
ground nutmeg
ground cloves
ground mustard
ground ginger
ground cumin
ground turmeric
garlic powder
onion powder
herbes de provence
dried basil
dried mint
dried thyme
dried rosemary
dried oregano
bay leaves
whole mustard seed
crushed rose petals
za'atar
sumac
peppercorns
peppermill
black pepper
chili powder

ESSENTIALS IF YOU'RE FEELING FANCY

chia seeds
vanilla beans
whole nutmeg
cinnamon sticks
rice bran oil
honeycomb
cider vinegar
wine vinegar
rose water
coconut milk
coconut sugar
saffron
flaxseed
fleur de sel
dried rose petals
dried lavender
whole cardamom pods
truffle honey

Save your carcasses from roast chicken—they're great to throw into chicken broth.

If you ever find yourself in the stinky predicament of having a fridge that smells of cooked foods and onions, etc., a good trick is to grab a potato or two, peel them, and leave them in the fridge to absorb the bad odors. Works like a charm.

READY
TO GO

Almost every Jewish woman I know has her own "aaaamazing" recipe for chicken broth. Well, mine is actually the best. Just kidding. What I will say is that mine is simple and allows room for making it your own. I don't add any aromatics other than fresh dill—and I leave the salt and pepper out until the end, when you can season to taste. Soaking the chicken in a mixture of white vinegar and water is a trick I use to help produce a cleaner, clearer broth. The acidity of the vinegar reacts with the protein and fat in the chicken in a magical way, and produces a pure, golden broth.

GOLDEN CHICKEN BROTH

1 whole chicken or chicken pieces, skin on and bone in

1 cup (250 ml) white vinegar

1 large yellow onion, skin on, washed

3 carrots, peeled

2 ribs celery

1 bunch dill

Lots of kosher salt and freshly ground black pepper

Place the chicken in a large bowl. Pour the vinegar and 1 cup (250 ml) cold water over the chicken, and let it sit for 5–10 minutes. Remove the chicken from the water and pat it dry with paper towels.

Place the chicken in a large pot. Add the onion, carrots, celery, and dill. Pour cold water over, filling the pot almost to the top. Warm over medium-high heat. Once the mixture starts bubbling, reduce the heat to medium-low and cook slowly for at least 2 hours. If you keep the heat low enough, there shouldn't be any scum on the surface. However, if there is a foamy buildup, simply skim it off using a slotted spoon. Allow the soup to simmer until it has reached a golden color that you're satisfied with. The longer it simmers, the darker it will get.

Use a large mesh strainer or skimmer to scoop out all of the chicken, veggies, and dill—discard the veggies and dill, but set the chicken aside on a dish to cool (we'll get back to the chicken in a bit). Once the solids are removed and all that remains is liquid, ladle the broth through a fine-mesh sieve, discarding all the grainy bits that are caught in the sieve. You should be left with a fragrant, golden-colored broth. Season to your liking with lots of salt and pepper.

Now, back to the chicken. You are left with a few choices on how to proceed. You can pull the chicken meat off the bones, shred it, and use it in your broth. Or, you can save it for another recipe, like Gingery Healing Broth (page 89), or add to your favorite salad recipe—I'd suggest Iceberg Wedges with Addictive Red-Roasted Chickpeas & Creamy Turmeric Drizzle (page 161).

MAKE-AHEAD TIP *Golden chicken broth should be cooled completely before storing in the fridge or freezer. It can be stored in the fridge for up to 1 week.*

CAN I FREEZE IT? *The broth can be frozen for up to 2 months. Thaw in the fridge overnight or on the counter for a few hours.*

HOW TO REHEAT *Reheat in a saucepan over medium heat for about 10 minutes.*

MAKES ABOUT 10 CUPS (2.5 L)

Vegetable broth is a key ingredient in so many recipes and can serve as the base for soup, rice, chicken, or fish dishes. Every few weeks, when it's time to clean out my fridge, instead of throwing away the veggies I haven't used that are on their way out, I create this beautiful broth. It's my idea of "kitchen recycling." You do not need to use the specific vegetables listed—use as much or as little as you have on hand. Unpeeled onions are the only must-include ingredient, as they release deep flavor and that gorgeous rich color.

QUICK VEGGIE BROTH

2   yellow onions, skin on, washed

4   carrots, peeled

2   ribs celery

1   fennel bulb, trimmed, cored, and cut into quarters

1   squash, peeled and cut into large chunks

2   turnips, peeled and cut in half

1   cup (90 g) mushrooms, brushed clean

1   sweet potato, peeled

1–2   regular potatoes, peeled

Fresh flat-leaf parsley or dill

Kosher salt and freshly ground black pepper

Combine all of the vegetables and herbs in a big pot and cover with cold water, filling up the pot three-fourths of the way. Bring to a boil over high heat and add 1 teaspoon salt and ½ teaspoon pepper. Reduce the heat to medium and simmer, uncovered, for 1 hour.

Use a large mesh strainer or skimmer to scoop out all of the veggies and herbs. Discard the herbs and set the veggies aside on a large dish to cool (we'll get back to them in a bit). Ladle the remaining liquid through a fine-mesh sieve, discarding all the grainy bits that are caught in the sieve. You should be left with a fragrant, golden-colored broth. Season to your liking with lots of salt and pepper.

Now, back to the veggies. I suggest using them in Aromatic Veggie Mash (page 160).

MAKE-AHEAD TIP *Quick veggie broth should be cooled completely before storing in the fridge or freezer. It can be stored in the fridge for up to 1 week.*

CAN I FREEZE IT? *The broth can be frozen for up to 2 months. Thaw in the fridge overnight or on the counter for a few hours.*

HOW TO REHEAT *Reheat in a saucepan over medium heat for about 10 minutes.*

MAKES ABOUT 10 CUPS (2.5 L)

IT'S NOT ALL ABOUT THE RECIPES—THEY ARE
JUST HALF THE BATTLE. IT'S ABOUT ORGANIZATION.
LET ME TELL YOU WHAT WORKS FOR ME: BEING
PREPARED. HAVING INGREDIENTS READY TO GO.

What do I use these onions in? The question should be, what don't I use these onions in? Caramelized onions will enhance almost any dish. Add to ground beef for delicious meatballs or meatloaf, mix into mashed potatoes or roasted vegetables, add to your soup base, or scatter over your roast leg of lamb. Place a dollop of caramelized onions over your grilled steak or rub them into your salmon before baking . . . I hope you see where I'm going with this. Caramelized onions are your secret weapon. And, I almost forgot the best part: You can prepare them and store them in the freezer so that you always have caramelized onions on hand.

CARAMELIZED ONIONS

2   **yellow onions**

2   **tablespoons neutral oil,
such as canola or rice bran oil**

    Kosher salt

Thinly slice the onions. In a large frying or sauté pan, heat the oil over medium-high heat. Once the oil is hot, add the onions, toss them in the oil, and season with ¼ teaspoon salt. Reduce the heat to medium and sauté the onions slowly, until translucent and dark brown, stirring with a wooden spoon throughout. This will take 15–20 minutes. The trick is to slowly cook the onions on medium heat to avoid burning them and to achieve a nice golden brown color, depth, and sweetness.

NOTE *This recipe is for 2 onions, but simply use it as a guide if you plan on making more. I often make this recipe with a 10-pound (4.5 kg) bag of onions! My thinking is, if I'm going to smell like onions, I might as well make it worthwhile.*

MAKE-AHEAD TIP *The onions can be sautéed and stored in a glass or plastic container or lock-top bag in the fridge for up to 1 week.*

CAN I FREEZE IT? *I recommend freezing in 1-tablespoon quantities. Place each portion in a small plastic freezer bag or in an ice-cube tray (reserved for savory purposes) and, once frozen, store the cubes in a lock-top plastic freezer bag for up to 3 months. Thaw overnight in the fridge or on the counter.*

MAKES ABOUT ¼ CUP (75 G) PER 2 ONIONS

Don't skip over this page just because you see the word "fried." Trust me—these golden, delicious gems are that secret ingredient you bite into and wonder: "What is that piece of heaven in my mouth?" This recipe is a good example of how a specific cooking method can transform an ingredient. Most people wouldn't feel euphoric while biting into a raw lemon slice, but once you blanch these thin, translucent slices, and then gently fry them in olive oil and sprinkle them with a touch of sea salt—you will change the entire experience. Instead of a sour flavor that makes you pucker, you get a rich, smooth, malty-lemony flavor.

FRIED LEMON SLICES

Kosher salt

1 firm lemon, sliced into very thin rounds, seeds removed

¼ cup (60 ml) light olive oil
Sea salt for sprinkling

Pour 5 cups (1.25 L) water into a medium pot and bring the water to a boil. Once the water is rapidly boiling, stir in a teaspoon of kosher salt. Carefully drop the lemon slices into the water and blanch for about 1 minute. Use a slotted spoon to fish the lemon slices out of the water, and drain them on a paper towel.

Meanwhile, in a frying pan, heat the oil over medium-high heat. Once the oil is hot (oil can splash and burn you—so be careful!), gently place the lemon slices into the oil. Cook the lemon slices, turning once, until the edges are golden brown and the flesh is a little sticky, about 2 minutes per side. Transfer the slices to a sheet of parchment paper, sprinkle with sea salt, and use as desired.

MAKE-AHEAD TIP *Fried lemon slices are best when used the same day you make them, but they can be stored in an airtight container or glass jar in the fridge for up to 4 days.*

CAN I FREEZE IT? *Fried lemon slices can be frozen for up to 3 months, and I recommend using the frozen slices in marinades or in recipes that will be cooked, rather than served fresh. They will work wonderfully in most fish and chicken dishes and roasts. Thaw on the counter until ready to use.*

MAKES ABOUT 10 SLICES

IT'S ALL ABOUT ORGANIZATION AND PREP—THE LITTLE STEPS ADD UP TO MAKE ALL THE DIFFERENCE IN YOUR KITCHEN.

JULIENNED CARROTS Use a julienne peeler to "peel" the entire carrot into strips. These carrots are great in salads, as a garnish, on their own with a simple vinaigrette, as part of a veggie platter, or served alongside hummus or your favorite dip.

WASHED & STORED KALE Tear the kale leaves away from the thick stems and veins in the center. Rinse under cold running water. Place the kale leaves on paper towels or kitchen towels to air-dry, patting with the paper towels to absorb any excess water. Place the paper towel-wrapped kale in large plastic lock-top bags in the fridge.

SLICED BEETS & RADISHES ON ICE Peel the beets and radishes and slice as thinly as possible. Place the slices in a container topped with a cup of ice. Store in the fridge for up to 3 weeks, draining the water and replacing the ice cubes every 4–5 days.

SHREDDED CABBAGE Peel away the rough outer layers of the cabbage. Cut the cabbage in half, lengthwise. Use a large vegetable peeler to shred the cabbage using fast downward strokes. Repeat with the other half. Wrap the shredded cabbage tightly in a paper towel and place in a plastic lock-top bag and store in the fridge for up to 2 weeks.

JULIENNED CARROTS →

WASHED & STORED KALE →

EVERYONE'S FAVORITE PICKLED RED ONIONS →

FRIED LEMON
SLICES

SLICED RADISHES
ON ICE

SLICED BEETS
ON ICE

SHREDDED
CABBAGE

These pickled red onions—crunchy and sour, with a hint of sweetness—are a fun condiment and go well with more mains than you might imagine. And unlike most pickles that take weeks to prepare, these take 5 minutes to assemble and will be "pickled" in an hour. I always have a jar in my fridge because my kids can't eat their burgers without them! It seems that everyone can't get enough. Don't forget to try the pickles on my Rustic Tartlets with Ricotta, Green Pesto & Pickled Onions (page 55).

EVERYONE'S FAVORITE PICKLED RED ONIONS

2 red onions, thinly sliced (about ⅛ inch/3 mm thick)

½ lime, sliced into thin rounds, seeds removed

1½ tablespoons sugar

½ cup (120 ml) apple cider vinegar

1½ teaspoons kosher salt

½ teaspoon whole black peppercorns

Boil 2 cups (500 ml) of water. Place the sliced onions in a large bowl and pour the hot water over the onions. Let the onions soften for 1–2 minutes and then drain. Place the onions in a glass jar. Add the lime rounds, sugar, vinegar, salt, and peppercorns. Close the jar and make sure the lid is tight. Shake the jar so that all of the ingredients are dispersed. Let the jar sit at room temperature for at least 1 hour or up 2 days. Store the onions in the fridge thereafter. To serve, drain the liquid.

MAKE-AHEAD TIP *Once the onions have marinated at room temperature for up to 2 days, they can be stored in a glass jar with a tight-fitting lid in the fridge for up to 3 weeks.*

MAKES ONE 16–FL OZ (500-ML) JAR

This recipe is a true essential. Having ready-to-go sauces, dips, and marinades stored in the fridge makes cooking so much quicker because you're always a step ahead. My friends often remark how amazing it is that I can whip up delicious finger foods and treats in no time when they pop by for a visit. I can't emphasize enough how easy it is to put together a beautiful platter using ingredients that you already have at home when the showstopper items (like this pesto) are ready and waiting.

RED PESTO

12 oil-packed sun-dried tomatoes, drained (oil reserved if desired)

1 cup (30 g) fresh basil leaves

1 clove garlic

1 chile, stemmed and seeded (optional)

1 tablespoon balsamic vinegar
Kosher salt and freshly ground black pepper

¼ cup (60 ml) extra-virgin olive oil or reserved sun-dried tomato oil

Place the tomatoes, basil, garlic, and chile, if using in the workbowl of a food processor (a mini food processor works well) and blitz until chopped finely. Add the vinegar, ½ teaspoon salt, and ¼ teaspoon pepper, and blitz again until a paste is formed. Transfer the paste to a glass jar and stir in the oil. Taste and adjust the seasoning to your liking.

MAKE-AHEAD TIP *Red pesto can be stored in a glass jar with a tight-fitting lid in the fridge for up to 2 weeks.*

CAN I FREEZE IT? *Pesto freezes well. I recommend freezing in 1-teaspoon portions in an ice-cube tray (reserved for savory purposes). Once frozen, store the cubes in a lock-top plastic freezer bag for up to 3 months. Thaw in the fridge overnight or on the counter.*

MAKES ONE 10–FL OZ (300-ML) JAR

When most people think of pesto, they think basil, garlic, and Parmesan. What a lot of people don't know is that pesto can actually be made with any greens or herbs. "Pesto" is derived from the Italian word *pestare,* meaning to "pound" or "crush." Whenever I see that the herbs and greens in my fridge are on the brink of going bad, I throw them into the food processor and make pesto! I use whatever I have on hand: basil, parsley, mint, arugula, and even kale. Mixing the different herbs and greens creates different bursts of flavor and complexity. My favorite combination is arugula, basil, and mint.

GREEN PESTO

3   cups (150 g) fresh leafy greens and herbs of your choice (I recommend basil, flat-leaf parsley, mint, arugula, kale—use one type or a combination), stemmed

1   clove garlic

1   chile, stemmed and seeded (optional)

2   tablespoons nuts or seeds of your choice (I recommend walnuts, almonds, pine nuts, sunflower seeds)
    Kosher salt and freshly ground black pepper

¼   cup (60 ml) extra-virgin olive oil

Place the herbs, garlic, chile, if using, and nuts or seeds in the workbowl of a food processor (a mini food processor works well) and blitz until chopped finely. Add ½ teaspoon salt and ¼ teaspoon pepper and blitz again until a paste is formed. Transfer the paste to a glass jar and stir in the oil. Taste and adjust the seasoning to your liking.

MAKE-AHEAD TIP *Pesto can be stored in a glass jar with a tight-fitting lid in the fridge for up to 2 weeks.*

CAN I FREEZE IT? *Pesto freezes well. I recommend freezing in 1-teaspoon portions in an ice-cube tray (reserved for savory purposes). Once frozen, store the cubes in a lock-top plastic freezer bag for up to 3 months. Thaw in the fridge overnight or on the counter.*

MAKES ONE 10–FL OZ (310-ML) JAR

Make this sauce. Make it again. Make it again and again until you memorize the recipe and no longer need to visit this page. It's that good—and it's that versatile. This is my go-to marinade. It pretty much works on any protein—lamb chops, veal chops, beef roasts, fish, tofu, or chicken. It's what I like to call my *"passe-partout"* or "my little black dress," because it works in every situation. Drizzle over roasted vegetables, stir into mashed potatoes, use as a salad dressing, toss into beans and legumes. Perhaps you have a package of chicken cutlets in the freezer? Marinate them in this luscious sauce. Do you have ground beef or chicken and aren't sure what to do with it? Mix in some of this sauce and form burgers or meatballs.

WINE, GRAINY DIJON & CITRUS SAUCE

¼ cup (60 ml) whole-grain Dijon mustard

⅔ cup (160 ml) red or white wine

2 tablespoons extra-virgin olive oil

Juice and flesh from 2 oranges or 1 grapefruit, or ½ cup (120 ml) fresh orange juice

1 teaspoon Worcestershire sauce

1 tablespoon pure maple syrup

1 tablespoon whole mustard seeds

1½ teaspoons dried thyme

1½ teaspoons dried rosemary

Kosher salt and freshly ground black pepper

Combine the mustard, wine, olive oil, orange juice, Worcestershire sauce, maple syrup, mustard seeds, thyme, rosemary, ½ teaspoon salt, and ¼ teaspoon pepper in a jar and close the lid tightly. Shake well to combine.

MAKE-AHEAD TIP *The sauce can be stored in a glass jar with a tight-fitting lid for up to 2 weeks.*

MAKES ONE 10–FL OZ (300-ML) JAR

How does a two-ingredient marinade sound? How about a two-ingredient dip? A two-ingredient rub? A two-ingredient condiment? A two-ingredient gourmet gift? I am sure you get my point. This recipe is all that, plus so much more. When you slow-roast the entire garlic bulb, the sharp flavors dissipate and emerge as a soft, deep, buttery garlic flavor. Rub into your raw chicken or meats before cooking. Drop a dollop onto grilled or roasted fish. Spread a thin layer on a slice of toasted sourdough for an easy tartine (page 82). I always put out a jar of this magic at my summer barbecues—it's heavenly on steaks and burgers, and a must for dipping fries! It's so good that my husband eats an entire roasted bulb on his own.

ROASTED GARLIC PASTE

2 **garlic bulbs**
2 **tablespoons light olive oil**
1 **tablespoon extra-virgin olive oil**

Preheat the oven to 425°F (220°C).

Cut a thin slice from the top (the wider part) of each garlic bulb. Tear off 2 sheets of aluminum foil and place a bulb in the center of each sheet. Drizzle the bulbs with the light olive oil and wrap them in the foil. Transfer the foil-wrapped bulbs to a small baking dish or a baking sheet lined with parchment paper, cut side up. Bake in the oven until the bulbs soften, 60–75 minutes. Let cool slightly and squeeze out all of the garlic paste, using a spoon to scrape it out, into a small glass jar. Pour the extra-virgin olive oil over the roasted garlic, and store in the fridge until ready to use.

MAKE-AHEAD TIP *Roasted garlic paste can be stored in the fridge for up to 2 weeks.*

CAN I FREEZE IT? *I recommend freezing in 1-tablespoon quantities. Place 1 tablespoon in a small plastic freezer bag to freeze for up to 3 months. Thaw in the refrigerator overnight or on the counter.*

MAKES ABOUT ¼ CUP (60 ML)

GREEN PESTO

RED PESTO

DILL & LEMON SIP

SPICY PEANUT SIP

ROASTED GARLIC
PASTE

THESE BASIC RECIPES ARE SO
EASILY INTERCHANGEABLE, THEY
CAN BE USED TO ENHANCE A
DISH OR AS THE MAIN FLAVORING
OF A MEAL. THE POSSIBILITIES
ARE ENDLESS.

TOASTED SESAME
MARINADE

WINE, GRAINY DIJON
& CITRUS SAUCE

HERB CHOP CHOP

What is a "sip"? It's a word that I made up. I couldn't decide if I should call this recipe a "sauce" or a "dip" because, honestly, it doubles as both. So, I settled on "sip." You may think it's tacky, but I think it's genius.

DILL & LEMON SIP

1   bunch fresh dill (look for bright colored dill with a "citrusy" scent)

1   lemon

1   tablespoon whole-grain Dijon mustard

2   cups (500 g) plain Greek yogurt or mayonnaise

Kosher salt and freshly ground black pepper

Chop the dill finely, including the stems and fine feathery leaves. Place in a medium bowl. Use a zester to zest the entire lemon into the same bowl. Cut the lemon in half and squeeze both halves into that same bowl. Add the mustard and the yogurt or mayonnaise. Mix together very well and season with ¾ teaspoon salt and ½ teaspoon pepper.

MAKE-AHEAD TIP *Dill and lemon sip can be stored in a glass jar with a tight-fitting lid in the fridge for up to 2 weeks.*

MAKES ONE 16–FL OZ (500-ML) JAR

Everyone needs a peanut "sip" (sauce and dip) in their recipe repertoire. It takes about three minutes to make, and if your pantry is stocked with all the essentials, you likely have all of these ingredients at home.

SPICY PEANUT SIP

¾   cup (200 g) smooth peanut butter

¼   cup (60 ml) rice vinegar

¼   cup (60 ml) hot water

⅓   cup (75 ml) soy sauce

3   tablespoons pure maple syrup

1½   teaspoons grated fresh ginger

1   clove garlic, minced

¼   cup (50 g) roughly chopped roasted peanuts

½   teaspoon red pepper flakes

In a medium bowl, combine the peanut butter, vinegar, hot water, soy sauce, maple syrup, ginger, garlic, peanuts, and red pepper flakes. Use a whisk to mix well, until the consistency is creamy. Use as desired.

MAKE-AHEAD TIP *Spicy peanut sip can be stored in a glass jar with a tight-fitting lid in the fridge for up to 2 weeks.*

MAKES ONE 10–FL OZ (300-ML) JAR

This is for all those people who complain about their herbs going bad before they have the chance to use them. Chopping the herbs and storing them in olive oil extends their shelf life by weeks. Use as you would use fresh herbs.

HERB CHOP CHOP

Fresh herbs of your choice, stems removed

Extra-virgin olive oil

Rinse the herbs under cold running water. Dry thoroughly, pressing the herbs into paper towels to remove all excess water. Use a large chef's knife, or an electric chopper, to finely chop all the herbs. Transfer the herbs to a small glass jar and cover with the olive oil. Close the lid of the jar and store in the fridge.

MAKE-AHEAD TIP *Herb chop chop can be stored in a glass jar with a tight-fitting lid in the fridge for up to 2 weeks.*

CAN I FREEZE IT? *Yes, and I recommend freezing in 1-tablespoon quantities. I like to freeze the portions in an ice-cube tray. Once frozen, store the cubes in a lock-top plastic freezer bag for up to 3 months. Thaw overnight in the fridge or on the counter.*

MAKES ABOUT 6 TABLESPOONS (90-ML) PER BUNCH OF FRESH HERBS

This is another versatile marinade that can work wonders in your everyday cooking. What I love most about this Asian-inspired mixture is that it is super easy to mix and match with many proteins and vegetables.

TOASTED SESAME MARINADE

½ cup (120 ml) soy sauce

¼ cup (60 ml) neutral oil such as canola or rice bran oil

1 tablespoon toasted sesame oil

½ cup (120 ml) rice vinegar

Juice of 1 lime

2 tablespoons honey

½ teaspoon ground ginger

1 tablespoon sesame seeds

¼ cup (35 g) ground black pepper

In a glass jar with a tight-fitting lid, combine the soy sauce, oils, vinegar, lime juice, honey, ginger, sesame seeds, and pepper. Shake well until blended.

MAKE-AHEAD TIP *Toasted sesame marinade can be stored in a glass jar with a tight-fitting lid in the fridge for up to 3 weeks.*

MAKES ONE 10–FL OZ (300-ML) JAR

The days of buying premade barbecue sauce are long gone. Not only because the prices have gotten so high, but also because the store-bought varieties contain so many artificial colors and ingredients to help give them a never-ending shelf life. But, you don't want to be eating food that can sit on a shelf for two years—it simply cannot be good for you. That's why you're going to love this recipe. Tangy but not spicy (so the little ones can enjoy it too), rich and flavorful, but not too sweet.

HOMEMADE BBQ SAUCE

¾ cup (160 g) dark brown sugar or coconut sugar

2½ teaspoons dry mustard

1 tablespoon paprika

1 cup (250 ml) ketchup

1 can (6 oz/180 g) tomato paste

½ cup (120 ml) red wine vinegar

1 tablespoon Worcestershire sauce
Kosher salt and freshly ground black pepper

In a medium bowl, combine the sugar, mustard, paprika, ketchup, tomato paste, vinegar, Worcestershire sauce, 1½ teaspoons salt, and 1 teaspoon pepper and mix well using a whisk. Continue whisking until the sugar has dissolved and the consistency of the sauce is even. Store in a large glass jar with a tight-fitting lid in the fridge.

MAKE-AHEAD TIP *Homemade barbecue sauce can be stored in a glass jar with a tight-fitting lid in the fridge for up to 4 weeks.*

MAKES ONE 10–FL OZ (300-ML) JAR

APPETIZERS & NIBBLES

We all know that nowadays we can't set out a big bowl of potato chips at a party like we used to. Like it or not, times have changed. We don't eat the way we used to. And, although I am by no means a "health cook," I do believe that when we know better, we do better. But I also happen to love crunchy foods to munch on. That's how I came up with this recipe: red, crunchy, spicy, and addictive chickpeas baked to perfection in a very hot oven. I often set out little bowls of these munchies alongside bowls of nuts and my guests go crazy for them! I always get the same reaction: "You made these!?" They're so good, you'd think they were from some fancy snack shop.

ADDICTIVE RED-ROASTED CHICKPEAS

1   **can (15 oz/430 g) chickpeas**
2   **tablespoons extra-virgin olive oil**
1   **tablespoon paprika**
½   **teaspoon cumin**
1   **teaspoon garlic powder**
½   **teaspoon red pepper flakes**
    Zest of 1 lemon
    Kosher salt and freshly ground black pepper

Preheat the oven to 425°F (220°C). Line a rimmed baking sheet with parchment paper.

Drain the chickpeas and rinse them under cold running water. Set out a large, clean kitchen towel and pour the chickpeas out onto the towel. Cover the chickpeas with paper towels and gently pat to absorb any excess water. Once the chickpeas are dry, transfer them to a large bowl. Add the oil, paprika, cumin, garlic powder, red pepper flakes, and lemon zest. Toss all together using your hands to ensure that all of the chickpeas are coated in the mixture. Season with 1 teaspoon salt and ½ teaspoon pepper and toss again.

Transfer the chickpeas and marinade to the baking sheet, spreading them out in an even, single layer. Bake in the oven, uncovered, for 30 minutes (if you remember, shake the pan once midway through cooking to ensure even cooking). Remove from the oven and let cool completely, about 30 minutes. Transfer to a serving bowl and enjoy.

MAKE-AHEAD TIP *Red-roasted chickpeas can be stored in a glass jar or plastic container with a tight-fitting lid for up to 1 week.*

MAKES ABOUT 2 CUPS (304 G)

Last-minute guests stopping by? This is the easiest and quickest recipe you could possibly prepare. I have a package of presliced smoked salmon in the fridge specifically for this recipe. It only takes five minutes to prepare and your guests will think you're a culinary sensation—I mean, who serves salmon carpaccio at home? The arugula can be swapped out for any fresh greens like spinach, kale, or even fresh basil leaves. Have fun with it. And, if you ever find yourself walking past the edible flowers at the supermarket, now you have a recipe you can use them in!

SMOKED SALMON CARPACCIO WITH JALAPEÑOS & LIME SAUCE

1   lb (500 g) thinly sliced smoked salmon

¼   cup (12 g) wild arugula

2   tablespoons chopped chives

1   jalapeño chile, stemmed and sliced very thinly

     Juice of 1 lime

3   tablespoons extra-virgin olive oil

     Freshly ground black pepper

     Edible flowers (optional)

Have a serving platter or dish approximately the size of a dinner plate ready. Arrange the smoked salmon neatly on the platter, covering the entire base of the surface. You may need to place 2 layers to use up all of the salmon. Sprinkle the arugula, chives, and jalapeño over the salmon.

In a small bowl, whisk together the lime juice, oil, and black pepper to taste. Just before serving, spoon all of this sauce over the top of the greens and salmon. Garnish with edible flowers, if using, and serve.

MAKE-AHEAD TIP *The salmon, arugula, chives, and jalapeño slices can be arranged on the serving dish up to 5 hours in advance and refrigerated. The lime sauce can be prepared up to 1 week in advance and stored in a glass jar with a tight-fitting lid in the pantry until ready to use.*

MAKES 6 SERVINGS

This recipe for marinated feta cheese is highly requested among my friends. It's easy to throw together this mix of creamy, salty feta cheese marinated with spicy jalapeños, shallots, and parsley in a lusciously lemony vinaigrette. I like to serve the marinated feta in small mason jars with fresh baguette slices, Addictive Red-Roasted Chickpeas (page 39), and a dry red wine.

MARINATED FETA

1   lb (500 g) firm feta cheese

2   jalapeño chiles, stemmed and thinly sliced

1   cup (250 ml) extra-virgin olive oil

    Zest and juice of 1 lemon

1   shallot, sliced finely

2   tablespoons finely chopped fresh flat-leaf parsley

1   teaspoon freshly ground black pepper

1   teaspoon sumac or paprika for garnish

Place the feta on a paper towel and pat dry on all sides, absorbing any excess liquid. Transfer the feta to a cutting board and use a large chef's knife to cut the feta into small dice, about ½ inch (12 mm) in size. Place the diced feta in a shallow dish that is big enough to hold the cheese in a single layer. Sprinkle the jalapeño slices over the feta. In a small bowl, stir together the oil, lemon zest and juice, shallot, parsley, and pepper and pour over the feta cheese. Cover the dish and marinate for 30 minutes unrefrigerated, or for up to 1 week in the fridge. Garnish with sumac before serving.

MAKE-AHEAD TIP *Marinated feta can be stored in the fridge for up to 1 week. The oil in the feta may solidify while refrigerated, so simply place the dish on the counter for 20 minutes before serving to allow the oil to liquefy.*

MAKES 6–8 SERVINGS

This is a twist on my pecan fig biscotti that so many people have made and loved. These paper-thin delicacies are a cross between a cracker and a cookie. The honey in the recipe gives them just a touch of sweetness, while the earthiness of the walnuts, rosemary, and lemon takes them to the next level. Serve the biscotti on their own with a nice glass of wine, and certainly with some beautiful cheeses on a cheese board (page 51).

WALNUT & ROSEMARY SAVORY BISCOTTI

3   **eggs**
2   **tablespoons honey**
     Zest of 1 lemon
½   **cup (60 g) chopped walnuts**
1   **tablespoon dried rosemary**
1¼   **cups (145 g) all-purpose flour**
1   **tablespoon whole-wheat flour**
     Kosher salt

Preheat the oven to 350°F (180°C). Line a loaf pan with parchment paper leaving enough excess paper to fold over the dough and set aside.

Use a handheld electric mixer, or a stand mixer fitted with the paddle attachment, to beat together the eggs, honey, and lemon zest. Mix at medium speed until well combined and creamy. Add the walnuts, rosemary, flours, and ½ teaspoon salt and mix on low speed just until combined.

Transfer the batter to the prepared loaf pan. Bring the sides of the parchment paper together and fold over to tighten so that the loaf takes on a more rounded shape. Bake in the oven for 45 minutes. Let cool completely, wrap in aluminum foil, and refrigerate overnight.

Preheat the oven to 300°F (150°C). Line a rimmed baking sheet with parchment paper.

Using a very sharp knife, cut the loaf into slices as thin as possible. Place the slices on the prepared baking sheet. Bake in the oven until golden, about 20 minutes.

MAKE-AHEAD TIP *Walnut and rosemary savory biscotti can be prepared 1 month ahead of time and stored in an airtight container in the pantry.*

CAN I FREEZE IT? *Biscotti freeze well in an airtight container for up to 1 month. Thaw on the counter; biscotti take only a few minutes to thaw.*

MAKES 6–8 SERVINGS

Those of you who have made my 5-Minute Hummus probably have the recipe memorized by now. This variation uses the same basic recipe but with the addition of parsley, jalapeño, and limes—three of my favorite green ingredients! This fresh and flavorful hummus is a major crowd-pleaser. If you want to tone down the heat, just skip the jalapeño. P.S. It lasts in the fridge for up to 2 weeks; if you're cooking for a crowd, do yourself a favor and double the recipe.

5-MINUTE SPICY GREEN HUMMUS

2   cans (15 oz/425 g each) chickpeas

1   heaping tablespoon tahini

1   handful of fresh flat-leaf parsley, including stems and leaves

1   jalapeño chile, stemmed and cut into chunks

1   clove garlic
    Zest and juice of 2 limes

¼   cup (60 ml) extra-virgin olive oil
    Kosher salt and freshly ground black pepper

Drain the chickpeas and rinse under cold running water. In the workbowl of a large food processor, combine the chickpeas, tahini, parsley, jalapeño, garlic, and lime zest and juice. Pulse until combined. While continuing to pulse, gradually add the oil, 1 tablespoon at a time, through the feed tube and continue to pulse until the desired consistency is reached. (Ask yourself: "Do I like it chunky or smooth?") Season generously with salt and pepper to your liking. Transfer the hummus to a serving bowl.

MAKE-AHEAD TIP *The hummus can be made and stored in a plastic or glass container with a tight-fitting lid in the fridge for up to 2 weeks. I recommend dividing the hummus up into smaller portions and storing it in several containers. The hummus will store better this way without too many spoons going in and out of the container.*

MAKES ABOUT 2 CUPS (500 ML)

There are two starring ingredients in this recipe: tomatoes and basil. The salt, pepper, and olive oil shouldn't count—they're a given. This recipe shows that when you start with fresh, seasonal produce, you really don't have to—and in fact, you shouldn't—do much to it. For a more composed look, you can slice the tomatoes as thinly as possible, arrange on a platter with the slices slightly overlapping, and slide a single basil leaf in between each tomato slice. Whenever I put out this platter, my family and friends talk about the tomatoes like they are pieces of art. The colors, flavors, and simplicity of the dish speaks for itself.

HEIRLOOM TOMATOES WITH BASIL

3   heirloom tomatoes,
    a mix of colors
1   bunch fresh basil, leaves
    picked
    Kosher salt and freshly ground
    black pepper
2   tablespoons extra-virgin
    olive oil

Use a serrated knife or sharp chef's knife to cut the tomatoes into wedges. Arrange the tomato wedges on a serving platter with the wedges slightly overlapping one another. Sprinkle with basil leaves. Just before serving, season the tomatoes with salt and pepper to your liking, and drizzle the oil over the top.

MAKE-AHEAD TIP *The tomatoes and basil can be arranged on the platter 1 hour before serving. Add the salt, pepper, and oil just before serving.*

MAKES 6 SERVINGS

WHEN YOU START WITH FRESH,
SEASONAL INGREDIENTS YOU REALLY
DON'T NEED TO DO MUCH WORK.
LET THE FOOD SPEAK FOR ITSELF.
YOU CAN'T GO WRONG WITH A
GORGEOUS TOMATO SALAD AND
A SUMMERY ROSÉ.

WINE & CHEESE BOARD

HOW DO YOU ENTERTAIN? More than any other question I get asked, people always request ideas for easy entertaining. They want to know what to serve for friends stopping by after work for a drink, or how to host a brunch without spending hours in the kitchen. What I've learned over time is that in people's minds, hosting means pressure. Boards make presenting food fun without much prep time. Everyone loves to graze, and a board feels like an indulgence with lots of items to choose from. It's a fresh, modern way to present food that looks like you went above and beyond for your guests. But it's all about assembling an enticing mix of fresh and savory items. Here are some of the elements I like to use:

GOOD-QUALITY HARD & SOFT CHEESES ♥ MARINATED FETA ♥ PISTACHIOS ♥ CASHEWS ♥ ROASTED ALMONDS ♥ DRIED APRICOTS ♥ FRUIT PRESERVES ♥ RAISINS ♥ CRACKERS ♥ GRAPE CLUSTERS ♥ STRAWBERRIES ♥ CHERRIES ♥ FRESH CURRANTS ♥ BLACKBERRIES OR RASPBERRIES ♥ CITRUS ♥ POMEGRANATE ♥ PASSION FRUIT ♥ FRESHLY SLICED BAGUETTE ♥ WALNUT & ROSEMARY SAVORY BISCOTTI ♥ HONEYCOMB ♥ PRUNES ♥ DARK CHOCOLATE ♥ DRIED FLOWERS ♥ OLIVES ♥ RED-ROASTED CHICKPEAS ♥ FIGS ♥ YOUR FAVORITE WINES ♥

FARMERS' MARKET BOARD

SETTING UP YOUR BOARD You will need a board as the base for your presentation; how convenient that you've already got a few cutting boards lying around! Use a board (turn it over to use the least-worn side), or any serving platter will work as well. The more mismatched the better! Start by collecting a few jars: mason jars, empty jam jars, olive jars—I save my condiment jars once they're used up, they come in super handy to hold dips or crudités. I also use any ramekins or small bowls, mixing and matching different shapes. Choose a combination of staple and seasonal produce. The key is to present each fresh item so it looks wild but not manicured. Boards convey an artisanal, I-just-threw-this-together look, and varying the heights and sizes of the different elements lends visual appeal.

CARROTS ♥ ASSORTED RADISHES ♥ FENNEL ♥ CUCUMBERS ♥ TOMATOES ON THE VINE ♥ SCALLIONS ♥ HARICOTS VERTS ♥ ASPARAGUS ♥ SUGAR SNAP PEAS ♥ SNOW PEAS ♥ HUMMUS ♥ CELERY ♥ NUTS ♥ EDIBLE FLOWERS ♥ FRESH HERBS ♥ ARTICHOKE HEARTS ♥ JALAPEÑOS ♥ FAVORITE DIPS & SIPS ♥ WALNUT & ROSEMARY SAVORY BISCOTTI ♥ ENDIVE ♥ FRESHLY SLICED BAGUETTE ♥ OLIVES ♥

I keep a package of prepared puff pastry sheets in my freezer at all times. The possibilities with puff pastry are endless. There is just so much you can make using this crispy, light, layered dough. With their golden flaky crust topped with a vibrant red pesto and speckled with cucumbers and olives, these tartlets are beautiful and delicious. Breakfast, lunch, dinner, or drinks—this is a go-to homemade quick fix that's sure to impress your guests and your appetite.

RUSTIC TARTLETS WITH RED PESTO, CUCUMBERS & OLIVES

1 **sheet frozen puff pastry dough, thawed in the fridge overnight or on the counter for 20 minutes**

1 **large egg**

½ **teaspoon honey**

1 **cup (250 ml) Red Pesto (page 25)**

2 **Kirby cucumbers, thinly sliced**

½ **cup (60 g) pitted olives of your choice**

Flaky sea salt

Preheat the oven to 400°F (200°C).

Lay out a sheet of parchment paper on your work surface. Unfold the puff pastry dough on the parchment sheet. Use a rolling pin to roll out the dough slightly, just to thin it out a bit. Use a sharp knife to cut the puff pastry dough into 10 equal-size squares. Transfer the parchment paper and pastry squares to a rimmed baking sheet, spacing the squares 1 inch (2.5 cm) apart.

In a small bowl, whisk together the egg and honey. Lightly brush the top of each pastry square with the egg mixture. Bake the puff pastry squares in the oven until they have puffed up and are golden brown, 15–20 minutes. Remove from the oven and let cool.

Once the pastry squares have cooled, spread a thin layer of red pesto over the center of each pastry square. Garnish with a few slices of cucumber and 1 or 2 olives. Sprinkle a few flakes of sea salt over the tops, and serve.

MAKE-AHEAD TIP *The pastry squares can be cut and baked up to 2 days in advance, but taste best on the day they were baked. Store baked pastry squares in a glass or plastic container with a tight-fitting lid in the pantry for up to 2 days. The tartlets are best when assembled just before serving.*

CAN I FREEZE IT? *Baked puff pastry squares (without topping) can be frozen in a glass or plastic container with a tight-fitting lid for up to 2 weeks.*

HOW TO REHEAT *Frozen baked puff pastry squares (without topping) can be reheated, uncovered, in a 350°F (180°C) oven for 5–8 minutes.*

MAKES 10 TARTLETS

I've always loved pairing ricotta and honey—the combination of creamy and sticky textures just works. The addition of green pesto and snappy pickled onions, though, really takes these delightful tartlets to the next level. You can bake the base of the tarts ahead of time, making these a terrific choice for last-minute entertaining—particularly if you have the pesto and pickled onions ready to go. Just before your guests arrive, assemble the tartlets.

RUSTIC TARTLETS WITH RICOTTA, GREEN PESTO & PICKLED RED ONIONS

1   sheet frozen puff pastry dough, thawed in the fridge overnight or on the counter for 20 minutes

1   large egg

½   teaspoon honey

1   cup (225 g) ricotta cheese

½   cup (120 ml) Green Pesto (page 27)

½   cup (50 g) Everyone's Favorite Pickled Red Onions (page 24), drained of their liquid

Lime slices (optional)

Red pepper flakes, to serve

Preheat the oven to 400°F (200°C).

Lay out a sheet of parchment paper on your work surface. Unfold the puff pastry dough on the parchment sheet. Use a rolling pin to roll out the dough slightly, just to thin it out a bit. Use a sharp knife to cut the puff pastry dough into 10 equal-size squares. Transfer the parchment paper and pastry squares to a rimmed baking sheet, spacing the squares 1 inch (2.5 cm) apart.

In a small bowl, whisk together the egg and honey. Lightly brush the top of each pastry square with the egg mixture. Bake the puff pastry squares in the oven until they have puffed up and are golden brown, 15–20 minutes. Remove from the oven and let cool.

Once the pastry squares have cooled, dollop 1 tablespoon of ricotta over the center of each. Use the back of a spoon to spread out a circle of ricotta over the center of the pastry. Drizzle a ½ teaspoon of pesto into the center of the ricotta circle. Top with a few slices of pickled onions and lime slices (if using) and sprinkle a few red pepper flakes over the tops.

MAKE-AHEAD TIP *The pastry squares can be cut and baked up to 2 days in advance, but they taste best on the day they were baked. Store baked pastry squares in a glass or plastic container with a tight-fitting lid in the pantry for up to 2 days. The tartlets are best when assembled just before serving.*

CAN I FREEZE IT? *Baked puff pastry squares (without topping) can be frozen in a glass or plastic container with a tight-fitting lid for up to 2 weeks.*

HOW TO REHEAT *Frozen baked puff pastry squares (without topping) can be reheated, uncovered, in a 350°F (180°C) oven for 5–8 minutes.*

MAKES 10 TARTLETS

THERE ARE SO
MANY POSSIBILITIES
WITH PUFF PASTRY
AND WHAT YOU CAN
DO WITH THIS LIGHT,
FLAKY DOUGH. A
PACKAGE OF PASTRY
DOUGH IS ALWAYS
IN MY FREEZER.

RUSTIC TARTLETS WITH
RICOTTA, GREEN PESTO
& PICKLED ONIONS

RUSTIC TARTLETS
WITH RED PESTO,
CUCUMBERS & OLIVES

This is what I like to call an "accidental recipe." It was a typical Thursday: I prepared my kids' favorite sticky chicken wings (I, for the record, won't eat chicken wings ever—just not my thing—but everyone seems to love them!). For some reason, I also decided to cook a box of angel hair pasta that I'd had in the pantry for ages. And so, it just happened. Instead of just lumping the pasta onto the plates, I decided to use some creative energy. I twisted the pasta into adorable little "nests" and topped them with hot chicken wings.

ANGEL HAIR NESTS TOPPED WITH STICKY CHICKEN WINGS

16 chicken wings, wing-tips removed, patted dry

1 cup (250 ml) Toasted Sesame Marinade (page 33)

2 tablespoons honey

1 package (16 oz/500 g) angel hair pasta

1 tablespoon extra-virgin olive oil

Kosher salt

Combine the chicken wings and marinade in a large lock-top plastic bag or container. Marinate the chicken wings for at least 30 minutes or up to 2 days.

Preheat the oven 350°F (180°C).

Remove the chicken wings from the marinade and transfer to a shallow baking dish. Discard the remaining marinade. Spread the wings out in a single layer and drizzle the honey over them. Bake the wings in the oven, uncovered, for 30 minutes. Remove from the oven and use tongs to flip the wings over in the baking dish. Return to the oven and bake for 20 minutes longer.

Meanwhile, cook the pasta according to package instructions. Once the pasta is cooked, drain. Drizzle the pasta with oil and toss in ½ teaspoon salt. Have 8 small serving bowls ready. Using tongs, grab about ¾ of a cup (85 g) of pasta and use a twisting motion to create a nest-like mound of pasta. Keep twisting until you can easily drop the pasta "nest" into a small serving bowl. Repeat with all your serving bowls. Remove the wings from the oven and place 2 wings over each pasta "nest." Serve right away.

MAKE-AHEAD TIP *Sticky chicken wings can be cooked up to 2 days ahead of time and refrigerated. Angel hair nests can be made up to 3 hours before serving. Form the oil-coated pasta into "nests" and place them on a parchment-lined baking sheet, cover with plastic wrap or aluminum foil, and store in a warm spot until ready to serve. There is no need to reheat the "nests"—the hot chicken wings should warm the pasta adequately.*

CAN I FREEZE IT? *Chicken wings can be frozen for up to 2 months. Thaw in the fridge overnight.*

HOW TO REHEAT *Reheat, uncovered, in a 325°F (165°C) oven for 10–15 minutes.*

MAKES 8 SERVINGS

I love, love, love the idea of cauliflower crust! Instead of a typical pizza crust made from flour, this is a crust made out of "cauliflower rice"—which is cauliflower that's been grated into teeny tiny pieces, resembling rice. Most of the recipes I've found for cauliflower crust are made with a lot of cheese and/or flour. I was determined to create a recipe that avoided both of those ingredients. I've added caramelized onions, which hold the dough together and add amazing flavor.

CAULIFLOWER & CARAMELIZED ONION CRUST

1 whole cauliflower or 2¼ cups (260 g) grated cauliflower

2 egg whites

½ cup (150 g) Caramelized Onions (page 20)

½ teaspoon garlic powder

¼ teaspoon dried basil
   Kosher salt and freshly ground black pepper

3 tablespoons extra-virgin olive oil

Pat the cauliflower dry. Remove all leaves, and cut into 4 even sections. Use a food processor fitted with the grater attachment to grate the cauliflower into pieces the size of rice grains, leaving any large, tough stems behind.

Bring a large pot of salted water to a boil. Put the grated cauliflower into the boiling water and let it cook for 2–3 minutes. Drain through a fine-mesh sieve. Measure out 2¼ cups (260 g) of grated cauliflower, transfer to a large bowl, and let cool.

Preheat the oven 375°F (190°C). Once the cauliflower has cooled, add the egg whites, caramelized onions, garlic powder, dried basil, ½ teaspoon salt, and a pinch of pepper. Use your hands to mix the ingredients together. Line a pizza pan or large baking sheet with parchment paper. Drizzle the parchment with 1 tablespoon of the olive oil, and use your hands to spread it over the paper. Spoon the cauliflower mixture onto the parchment and use your hands to spread it out and flatten it into a round, thin pizza crust. Drizzle the remaining 2 tablespoons olive oil over the crust and spread it over the top.

Bake in the oven until the crust is golden and crisp, about 30 minutes. Remove from the oven and let cool completely before adding toppings of your choice. I recommend spreading the crust with pesto and topping with torn pieces of fresh mozzarella; bake an additional 5 minutes, or until the toppings are baked to your liking.

MAKE-AHEAD TIP *Cauliflower pizza crust can be baked up to 6 hours in advance and kept at room temperature until ready to use.*

HOW TO REHEAT *Reheat, uncovered, in a 350°F (180°C) oven for about 10 minutes.*

MAKES ONE 13-INCH (33-CM) PIZZA CRUST

Charcuterie—which includes pork-based prosciutto, terrines, and pâtés—is not exactly what comes to mind when you think "kosher". But in fact, kosher charcuterie has been popular in Israel and France for many years, and nowadays non-pork and kosher options for bacon and pepperoni, prosciutto, and pâté can be found readily. That's great news, because this recipe takes just a few minutes to prepare and makes a modern, delectable appetizer for your next dinner party.

TWICE-COOKED CHARCUTERIE WITH SWEET DIJON DIPPING SAUCE

1–2 lb (500 g–1 kg) of your favorite kosher charcuterie, sliced (try beef "bacon," pepperoni, or spicy salami or lamb or duck "prosciutto")

FOR THE SWEET DIJON DIPPING SAUCE

1 tablespoon apricot or peach jam

½ cup (120 ml) whole-grain Dijon mustard

Pinch of freshly ground black pepper

Preheat the oven to 400°F (200°C). Line 1 or 2 rimmed baking sheets with parchment paper.

Lay the charcuterie meat on the parchment paper in a single layer, leaving ½ inch (12 mm) between each slice. Place in the oven and bake until crispy and bubbling hot, 10–15 minutes.

Meanwhile, prepare the sweet Dijon dipping sauce: In a small pot, melt the jam slightly over medium heat until just softened. Transfer to a small bowl and stir in the mustard and pepper until well combined.

Remove the meat from the oven and transfer to a platter or board. Serve with the dipping sauce.

MAKE-AHEAD TIP *Cured meats should be baked only just before serving to ensure that they crisp up and do not dry out. The dipping sauce may be made and stored in a glass jar or container with a tight-fitting lid for up to 1 week. Bring the sauce to room temperature before serving.*

ABOUT 4 SERVINGS PER 1 LB (500 G) CHARCUTERIE

BRUNCH

The only problem with these overnight oats is that they never make it overnight. *Somebody* in my family likes to finish them off midway through the evening. My neighbors probably wonder why they often hear me yelling: "They're called *overnight* oats, Jon!" The hype behind overnight oats is that the oats "cook" overnight in the fridge as they steep in liquid (the liquid can be yogurt, milk, or anything that the oats will absorb). This recipe includes yummy vanilla extract and frozen berries, but feel free to play around with the recipe and personalize it. There really is no formula for this one. But one thing is for certain: recipes like this one are keepers—a breakfast or brunch staple that can be prepared the night before and doesn't require any cooking or heating. Sold!

VANILLA-BERRY OVERNIGHT OATS

3   cups (750 g) plain yogurt, regular or Greek will do (you may use flavored yogurt if you like)

2   tablespoons pure vanilla extract

2   tablespoons milk, coconut milk, or almond milk

1   tablespoon chia seeds (optional)

2   cups (200 g) old-fashioned oats
    Kosher salt

2   cups (380 g) frozen mixed berries
    Pure maple syrup for drizzling

Wash and dry six 6-oz (180-ml) jars with lids, and set aside. In a large bowl, stir together the yogurt, vanilla, milk, and chia seeds, if using. Add the oats and ½ teaspoon salt, and stir well. Place 3 tablespoons of the mixture into the base of each jar. Scoop 3 tablespoons of frozen berries over the oats and repeat the layering by adding 3 more tablespoons of oats over the berries. Add another layer of berries over the oats and drizzle with maple syrup. Cover the jars with lids and refrigerate for at least 4 hours or preferably overnight before eating.

MAKE-AHEAD TIP *Vanilla-berry overnight oats should be prepared ahead and refrigerated for at least 4 hours or preferably overnight. Overnight oats can be refrigerated for up to 2 days. Serve directly from the fridge to the table.*

MAKES SIX 6–FL OZ (180-ML) JARS

What you have here, my friends, is your all-in-one breakfast of champions. Sautéed spinach and kale cooked with onions, garlic, and herbs, speckled with chickpeas, studded with creamy cheese, and topped with baked eggs. Flavored with fresh lemon and za'atar. Drizzled with good olive oil and dusted with red pepper flakes. Sounds like a good idea to me. And, even though this recipe is in the brunch chapter, please feel free to make it any time of day. God knows I have.

GREEN EGGS & GARBANZOS

2 tablespoons light olive oil

1 yellow onion, diced

1 teaspoon Roasted Garlic Paste (page 29) or 2 cloves garlic, minced

1 tablespoon Herb Chop Chop (page 33; optional)

1 box (10 oz/280 g) frozen chopped spinach, thawed and drained well of excess liquid

3 cups (225 g) Washed and Stored Kale (page 22)

1 can (15 oz/430 g) chickpeas, drained and rinsed

Juice of 1 lemon

1 tablespoon za'atar

Kosher salt and freshly ground black pepper

½ cup (60 g–110 g) crumbled feta or ricotta cheese

6 large eggs

Extra-virgin olive oil, to serve

Red pepper flakes, to serve

In a large sauté pan, heat the oil over medium-high heat. Add the onion and sauté until translucent, about 5 minutes. Add the garlic and herbs, if using, and cook for 2 minutes longer. Stir in the spinach and kale and sauté until softened, about 3 minutes. Add the chickpeas, lemon juice, za'atar, 1 teaspoon salt, and ½ teaspoon black pepper, and toss all together. Taste and adjust the seasoning to your liking.

Reduce the heat to low and bring the mixture to a simmer. Place a few mounds of cheese over the top of the greens. Use a wooden spoon to form 6 craters (indentations) in the greens; this is where the cracked eggs will be dropped. Working with one egg at a time, crack an egg into a small bowl (to catch any loose shells), and then pour it into the crater. Repeat with the remaining eggs. Raise the heat to medium, cover the sauté pan, and cook for 4 minutes. Uncover and cook for a few minutes longer, depending on the doneness of the eggs. The goal is to have the whites slightly firm but the yolks still runny. Remove from the heat, drizzle with extra-virgin olive oil, and sprinkle with red pepper flakes. Serve right away.

MAKE-AHEAD TIP *The greens and chickpeas can be kept in the sauté pan on the counter for up to 2 hours until ready to reheat and add the cheese and eggs.*

MAKES 6–8 SERVINGS

This is one of those recipes that sounds super complicated but is actually very simple. I asked around to see if my friends thought I should include it and the response was a unanimous "Yes!" Using store-bought babka makes this recipe as easy as 1-2-3, but if you happen to bake your own babka, definitely use it! Before serving, I transfer the slices into a loaf pan and line them up in a row so they go back to forming the original "loaf" shape to surprise guests with presliced chewy goodness.

1-2-3 BABKA FRENCH TOAST LOAF

¼ cup (4 tablespoons/60 g) unsalted butter, plus more for greasing

1 babka loaf or cinnamon loaf, about 15 oz (430 g)

3 large eggs

⅓ cup (75 ml) heavy cream

1 tablespoon vanilla extract or seeds from 1 vanilla bean

½ teaspoon ground cinnamon

Preheat the oven to 300°F (150°C). Grease a loaf pan with butter and set aside. Line a large rimmed baking sheet with parchment paper.

Use a large chef's knife to cut the babka into slices 1 inch (2.5 cm) thick. Lay the slices out on the prepared baking sheet, and set aside.

In a large bowl, whisk together the eggs, cream, vanilla, and cinnamon. Dip the babka slices, 1 slice at a time, in the egg mixture. Coat both sides for about 30 seconds, allowing the babka slice to absorb some of the egg mixture without getting too soggy or falling apart. Repeat with all of the slices, placing them back on the parchment-lined baking sheet while you finish up.

In a large sauté pan, heat 1 tablespoon of butter over medium-high heat. Once the butter is melted, add 2 slices of babka and fry, turning once, 1–2 minutes per side until golden. Transfer the browned slices to the prepared loaf pan, lining the slices up to re-create the original loaf shape. Continue heating 1 tablespoon of butter at a time in the pan and browning the babka slices in batches, 2 slices at a time, and transferring them to the loaf pan. Use all of the French toast slices to fill the loaf pan.

If serving right away, place the loaf pan in the oven, uncovered, for 5–7 minutes. This will heat all the slices up to the same temperature and make them toasty.

MAKE-AHEAD TIP *Babka French toast loaf can be prepared up to 2 days in advance and stored, covered, in the refrigerator. If preparing ahead of time, do not bake in the oven before refrigerating (skip the last step in the recipe).*

CAN I FREEZE IT? *Babka French toast loaf can be stored in the freezer for up to 1 month. If preparing ahead of time, do not bake in the oven before freezing (skip the last step in the recipe).*

HOW TO REHEAT *Babka French toast loaf can be reheated, uncovered, in a 400°F (200°C) oven for 10 minutes just before serving. Frozen French toast loaf can be thawed in the fridge overnight and reheated as indicated in the recipe above.*

MAKES 8–10 SERVINGS

KEEP YOUR TABLE
DÉCOR SIMPLE,
AIRY, AND CLEAN.
REMEMBER, THE
FOOD IS PART OF
THE OVERALL LOOK.
SET YOUR TABLE
TO HIGHLIGHT THE
BEAUTY OF YOUR
DELICIOUS FOOD.

Whenever I host a brunch, I set out one or two pound-cake loaves, thickly sliced, on wooden boards and serve some chic butters or jams on the side. I've never had a slice of this lemon berry loaf left over! Everyone goes wild for it—it's moist, colorful, and simply delicious. I love the fact that I can bake this loaf up to a month in advance and store it in the freezer until I need it. And, the lemon butter takes just a few minutes to mix together, but truly adds the finishing touch.

LEMON & BURSTING BERRY LOAF WITH TART LEMON BUTTER

FOR THE LEMON BERRY LOAF

- 2 cups (230 g) all-purpose flour
- 1½ teaspoons baking powder
- ¾ teaspoon kosher salt
- ½ cup (1 stick/115 g) unsalted butter, softened
- 1 cup (200 g) sugar
- 2 large eggs
- 2 teaspoons lemon zest
  Juice of 1 lemon
- ½ cup (125 g) yogurt (plain or vanilla)
- 2 cups (380 g) frozen or fresh berries, any variety

FOR THE LEMON BUTTER

- ½ cup (1 stick/115 g) unsalted butter, softened
  Zest of 2 lemons
- 1 teaspoon raw sugar

Preheat the oven to 350°F (180°C). Line a loaf pan with parchment paper and set aside.

To prepare the lemon berry loaf, in a medium bowl, whisk together the flour, baking powder, and salt. Set aside. In a stand mixer fitted with the paddle attachment, beat together the butter and sugar on medium speed. Add the eggs one at a time, beating each until incorporated, and stir in the lemon zest and juice. Add the yogurt and mix until all is combined. With the mixer on low speed, add the dry ingredients and mix just until combined. Use a spatula to fold in the berries. Pour the batter into the prepared loaf pan.

Bake until a toothpick inserted in the center comes out clean, 60–70 minutes. Place on a rack and let cool completely before removing from the pan.

To prepare the lemon butter, use an electric mixer to beat the butter until soft, add the lemon zest, and mix until combined. Transfer to a small serving bowl and sprinkle the raw sugar over the top.

Serve the loaf cut into thick slices with lemon butter.

MAKE-AHEAD TIP *The lemon berry loaf can be wrapped tightly in plastic wrap and stored in a cool, dry place for up to 2 days. The lemon butter can be made and refrigerated for up to 5 days.*

CAN I FREEZE IT? *The lemon berry loaf can be made ahead and stored in the freezer for up to 1 month. Thaw on the counter overnight. Do not freeze the lemon butter.*

MAKES 1 LOAF

You've probably skimmed the ingredient list to figure out what the 'Z' stands for: zucchini. I didn't want to spell it out in the title because I was worried that some of you would skip this recipe. If you love zucchini bread, I guarantee that you'll love this version. But if you need some convincing, don't think of zucchini as the main flavor here. Instead, embrace the fact that the zucchini serves as flavorless moisture in the recipe. If you prefer muffins, this batter yields a dozen muffins; bake for 20–25 minutes.

CHOCOLATE CINNAMON 'Z' LOAF WITH CINNAMON SWIRL BUTTER

1½   cups (175 g) all-purpose flour

½   teaspoon baking powder

½   teaspoon baking soda

½   teaspoon kosher salt

1   tablespoon ground cinnamon

½   teaspoon ground nutmeg

½   cup (120 ml) canola or rice bran oil

½   cup (100 g) light or dark brown sugar

1   large egg

1   teaspoon vanilla extract

1   cup (115 g) finely grated zucchini (about 1 small zucchini)

1   cup (180 g) mini chocolate chips or chopped chocolate of your choice

½   cup (60 g) chopped walnuts (optional)

2   teaspoons granulated sugar mixed with 2 teaspoons ground cinnamon

FOR THE CINNAMON SWIRL BUTTER

½   cup (1 stick/115 g) unsalted butter, softened

½   teaspoon ground cinnamon

¼   teaspoon granulated sugar

Preheat the oven to 350°F (180°C). Grease and line a loaf pan with parchment paper and set aside.

In a large bowl, combine the flour, baking powder, baking soda, salt, cinnamon, and nutmeg. Whisk to combine. In a stand mixer fitted with the paddle attachment, beat the oil and brown sugar on medium speed for 2 minutes. Add the egg and vanilla and mix on medium speed until creamy. Use a spatula to stir in the zucchini. Add the dry ingredients and mix on low speed just until all the ingredients are combined. Stir in the chocolate and nuts, if using. Do not overmix.

Pour the batter into the prepared loaf pan. Sprinkle the cinnamon sugar evenly over the top of the loaf. Bake until a toothpick inserted in the center comes out clean, 45–55 minutes. Remove from the oven and let cool completely.

To prepare the cinnamon swirl butter, use an electric mixer to beat the butter until soft. Add the cinnamon and sugar and mix until combined. Transfer to a small serving bowl and use a knife to mold the butter into a swirly shape.

MAKE-AHEAD TIP *The chocolate cinnamon loaf can be stored in an airtight container for up to 4 days. The cinnamon swirl butter can be made ahead and refrigerated for up to 5 days.*

CAN I FREEZE IT? *The chocolate cinnamon loaf can be made 1 month ahead and frozen in lock-top plastic bags. Thaw on the counter for about an hour. Do not freeze the cinnamon swirl butter.*

MAKES 1 LOAF

LEMON & BURSTING
BERRY LOAF →

I LOVE THAT I
CAN BAKE THESE
LOAVES UP TO A
MONTH IN ADVANCE
AND FREEZE THEM
UNTIL I'M READY TO
SERVE THEM.

CHOCOLATE CINNAMON
'Z' LOAF

I am a Medjool date snob. I've been known to travel far and wide to get a good box of Medjool dates. (There's a famous story among my friends about me asking my husband for his credit card at a shiva house in Great Neck, Long Island, after biting into the most delicious date of my life.) Look for plump, moist dates that appear dark brown and shiny. I store my dates in small plastic bags in the freezer and take them out as needed. They'll thaw in just a few minutes once removed from the freezer.

MEDJOOL DATE SQUARES WITH QUINOA, PECANS & SOUR CHERRIES

About 25 soft, plump Medjool dates

- ¼ cup (45 g) uncooked quinoa
- ½ cup (50 g) old-fashioned oats
- 1 cup (115 g) chopped pecans
- ⅓ cup (75 ml) pure maple syrup
- 1 teaspoon vanilla extract
- ¼ cup (60 ml) warm water
- 1 cup (155 g) frozen pitted sour cherries, thawed

Fleur de sel or other sea salt

Preheat the oven to 375°F (190°C). Line a 9-by-11-inch (23-by-28-cm) rectangular baking pan with parchment paper, leaving a 2-inch (5-cm) overlap on each end of the pan, and set aside.

Use your fingertips to gently open up each date and remove the pits. Place the pitted dates in a large bowl. If the dates are soft enough, you can use your hands to mush them all together and form a paste. (If the dates need to be softened, you may place them in the microwave for 1 minute, or transfer them to a sauté pan and heat slightly over medium heat. Once they heat up a little bit, they will be soft enough to mash with your hands.)

Add the quinoa, oats, pecans, maple syrup, vanilla, and water to the dates. Use your hands to mix, making sure that all the ingredients are dispersed evenly. Fold in the cherries. Transfer the mixture to the prepared dish and press down firmly into a flat, even layer. (You may need to wet your hands with cold water to make this easier.) Sprinkle 1 teaspoon salt over the top.

Bake in the oven, uncovered, for 20 minutes. Remove from the oven and let cool completely. Unmold in one piece using the excess parchment paper as handles to lift the date rectangle out of the pan. Use a large chef's knife to cut into evenly sized squares.

MAKE-AHEAD TIP *The date squares can be made up to 4 days in advance and stored in an airtight container in the pantry.*

CAN I FREEZE IT? *The date squares can be frozen in an airtight container or in lock-top plastic freezer bags for up to 1 month. Thaw on the counter; they will take only about 20 minutes to thaw, though I've noticed that some people like to eat them straight from the freezer.*

MAKES ABOUT 20 SQUARES

This recipe is wonderful for your small-batch, on-the-spot cooking moment. Toasting the oats and almonds on the stove top with just a little bit of butter and maple syrup will fill your home with a warm, mouthwatering aroma. The stove-top "baked apples" soaked in tea offer a delicious change to the usual granola pairing. I set up all my prep for this recipe before my family arrives at the breakfast table, and then I quickly whip up these special bowls while everyone waits patiently.

STOVE-TOP TOASTED GRANOLA & WARM APPLE BOWLS

FOR THE APPLES

- 1 tablespoon coconut oil or unsalted butter
- 3 apples (any variety), peeled, cored, and very thinly sliced
- 1 tablespoon coconut sugar or brown sugar
- ½ cup (120 ml) of your favorite hot herbal tea (I suggest mild flavored teas, such as chamomile or green tea)

FOR THE GRANOLA

- 1 cup (100 g) old-fashioned oats
- ¼ cup (25 g) skin-on sliced almonds
- 1 tablespoon coconut oil or unsalted butter
- 3 tablespoons pure maple syrup
  Kosher salt
  Ground cinnamon for sprinkling

Have 6 small serving bowls or mason jars handy.

To prepare the apples, in a large sauté pan, melt the coconut oil over medium-high heat. Add the apples and sauté for 2 minutes. Sprinkle the sugar over the apples and pour over the tea. Cook over high heat until the apples have absorbed most of the liquid and softened slightly, 5 minutes. Remove from the heat and divide the apples equally among 6 bowls or mason jars.

To prepare the granola, return the same sauté pan to the stove top and heat over medium-low heat. Add the oats and almonds and toast for a few minutes, until fragrant. Add the coconut oil, maple syrup, and ½ teaspoon salt. Sauté and stir for 2 minutes longer. Remove from the heat and divide the oats evenly over each of the apple bowls. Sprinkle a pinch of cinnamon over the top of each bowl. Serve right away.

MAKE-AHEAD TIP *The granola and apple bowls can be made up to 4 hours in advance and stored in oven-safe serving bowls or mason jars on the counter.*

HOW TO REHEAT *The granola and apple bowls can be reheated, uncovered, in a 300°F (150°C) oven for 10 minutes.*

MAKES 6 SERVINGS

Many people have their own version of shakshuka. This is mine. I grew up eating it and can recall my grandmother quickly preparing me a plate of shakshuka when I was a young girl visiting her in Israel. Though I know many people like to add cheese and veggies, I keep mine simple—tomatoes, onions, garlic, a few spices, and eggs. It tastes like home to me, and I like it that way.

RED SHAKSHUKA, MY WAY

1 can (28 oz/800 g) whole peeled tomatoes (do not drain)

2 tablespoons light olive oil

1 onion, diced

1 teaspoon Roasted Garlic Paste (page 29) or 2 cloves garlic, minced

2 jalapeño chiles, stemmed and thinly sliced (optional)

1 teaspoon cumin

1 teaspoon paprika

Kosher salt and freshly ground black pepper

6 large eggs

Pour the entire can of tomatoes and their juices into a large bowl. Roll up your sleeves, stick your hands in the bowl, and start squeezing! Squeeze and crush until all of the tomatoes are broken up into smaller pieces and what you have left is a thick, chunky sauce. Set aside.

In a large sauté pan, heat the oil over medium-high heat. Add the onion and sauté until translucent, about 5 minutes. Add the garlic paste and jalapeños, if using, and cook for 2 minutes longer. Stir in the cumin, paprika, 1 teaspoon salt, and ½ teaspoon pepper. Stir all together and cook for a few minutes longer.

Pour the tomato sauce over the onion mixture, stir, and bring to a boil. Reduce the heat to low and simmer, stirring constantly, until thickened, 6–8 minutes. Now your sauce is ready. (At this point, you may remove the sauce from the heat and let it cool. The sauce may be stored in the fridge for later use.)

Use a wooden spoon to form 6 craters (indentations) in the sauce; these are where the cracked eggs will be dropped. Working with one egg at a time, crack the egg into a small bowl (to catch any loose shells), and pour it into a crater. Repeat with the remaining eggs. Raise the heat to medium, cover the sauté pan, and cook for 4 minutes. Uncover and cook for a few minutes longer, depending on the doneness of the eggs. The goal is to have the whites slightly firm but the yolks still runny. Remove from the heat and serve right away.

MAKE-AHEAD TIP *The tomato sauce can be prepared and kept in the saute pan on the counter for up to 2 hours until ready to reheat and add to the eggs. It can be stored in a glass or plastic jar with a tight-fitting lid in the fridge for up to 1 week.*

CAN I FREEZE IT? *The tomato sauce can be made in advance and stored in a glass or plastic jar with a tight-fitting lid in the freezer for up to 1 month. Thaw in the fridge overnight or on the counter for a few hours.*

HOW TO REHEAT *Reheat on the stove top over medium heat for about 10 minutes.*

MAKES 6–8 SERVINGS

ESSENTIAL TARTINES

Tartines, or open-faced toasts, have made their way onto breakfast menus everywhere. It started with avocado toasts, and now "beet toasts" are popping up all over town. What I love about tartines is that there are no rules when it comes to toppings. The recipes below are my preferred topping combinations and use a few basic essentials that I almost always have on hand (and I encourage you to have as well—the recipes are in the first chapter). Storing a loaf of your favorite bread in the freezer is always a good idea so you can make tartines at any time. You definitely can and should experiment with toppings to your liking. I'm offering these three combinations to you as mere inspiration but really, have fun with these and mix and match!

TUSCAN BEANS WITH ROASTED GARLIC & FRIED LEMON SLICES

Eight ½-inch (12-mm) slices of your favorite bread (sourdough, spelt, rustic, miche, levain) or flatbread crackers

2 tablespoons Roasted Garlic Paste (page 29) or 6 cloves garlic, minced

1 can (15 oz/430 g) organic white beans, drained, rinsed, and patted dry

Extra-virgin olive oil for drizzling

8 Fried Lemon Slices (page 21)

Place the bread slices on a baking sheet and toast lightly on both sides under the broiler (or use a toaster). Spread a thin layer of the garlic paste on each piece of bread. Spoon 1 tablespoon of beans over the paste and drizzle about ¼ teaspoon of oil over the beans. Garnish with a fried lemon slice that has been sprinkled with a few flakes of sea salt over the top. Serve right away.

MAKE-AHEAD TIP *Tartines should be made no more than 30 minutes before serving. Roasted Garlic Paste (page 29) and Fried Lemon Slices (page 21) may be prepared in advance.*

MAKES 8 TARTINES

LABNE ZA'ATAR WITH SLICED BEETS & RADISHES

Eight ½-inch (12-mm)
slices of your favorite bread
(sourdough, spelt, rustic, miche,
levain) or flatbread crackers

1   cup (250 g) labne

¼   cup (25 g) za'atar

Extra-virgin olive oil

About 10 Sliced Beets and
Radishes on Ice (page 22),
patted dry

Fleur de sel or other sea salt

Place the bread slices on a baking sheet and toast lightly on both sides under the broiler (or use a toaster). Drizzle 2 tablespoons of labne over the center of each piece of bread. Sprinkle a teaspoon of za'atar over the labne and drizzle about ½ teaspoon of oil over the za'atar. Garnish with beets and radishes, and sprinkle a few flakes of sea salt over the tops. Serve right away.

MAKE-AHEAD TIP *Tartines should be made no more than 30 minutes before serving. Sliced Beets and Radishes on Ice (page 22) may be prepared in advance.*

MAKES 8 TARTINES

CARAMELIZED ONIONS WITH CHERRY TOMATOES, DILL & LEMON SIP

Eight ½-inch (12-mm)
slices of your favorite bread
(sourdough, spelt, rustic, miche,
levain) or flatbread crackers

½   cup (120 ml) Dill and Lemon
Sip (made with yogurt, page 32)

½   cup (50 g) Caramelized
Onions (page 20)

½   cup (90 g) cherry tomatoes,
any variety, halved

Fleur de sel or other
sea salt

Place the bread slices on a baking sheet and toast lightly on both sides under the broiler (or use a toaster). Spread a thick layer of the dill and lemon sauce on each piece of bread. Spoon ½ tablespoon of caramelized onions over the yogurt, scatter a few halved tomatoes on each tartine, and sprinkle a few flakes of sea salt over the tops. Serve right away.

MAKE-AHEAD TIP *Tartines should be made no more than 30 minutes before serving. Dill & Lemon Sip (made with yogurt, page 32) and Caramelized Onions (page 20) may be prepared in advance.*

MAKES 8 TARTINES

THESE TARTINES FEATURE INGREDIENTS
FROM MY "READY TO GO" CHAPTER AND
CAN BE PREPARED IN JUST A FEW MINUTES.
THEY ARE ALWAYS A CROWD-PLEASER.
SIMPLE + BEAUTIFUL = DELICIOUS.

QUICK STOVE-TOP MAINS

This is more than just an amazingly fragrant soup: it's an all-in-one pot meal. Chicken, veggies, and noodles in a light, gingery-garlic golden broth really nourishes in more than one way. I know that traditionally chicken matzo ball soup is meant to be the go-to when you're feeling under the weather, but I opt to go for this instead—the fresh ginger gives me the kick that I need to get back into shape.

GINGERY HEALING BROTH WITH MUSHROOMS, CARROTS, LEEKS & KALE

1 tablespoon neutral oil (canola, vegetable, avocado, rice bran)

1 tablespoon grated fresh ginger

1 tablespoon grated fresh garlic

2 cups (460 g) thinly sliced mushrooms (you may use a variety, including portobello, oyster, white button, baby bella, shiitake)

4 leeks, trimmed and sliced crosswise into thin rounds, then rinsed and patted dry
Kosher salt and freshly ground black pepper

8 cups (2 L) vegetable or chicken stock (if you don't have stock handy, you may also use water)

⅓ cup (75 ml) soy sauce

2 cups (360 g) shredded cooked chicken (you may use leftover roast chicken or grilled chicken, white or dark meat or a combination)

2 carrots, peeled and julienned
Half of a 7-oz (220-g) package udon noodles

1 handful of Washed & Stored Kale (page 22), torn into small pieces
Drizzle of toasted sesame oil (optional)
Fresh red chile, stemmed and very thinly sliced (also optional—if you, like me, love the heat)

In a large pot, heat the oil over medium-high heat. Add the ginger, garlic, and mushrooms. Use a wooden spoon to keep the ingredients moving in the hot oil. Sauté for 3 minutes, then add the leeks. Cover and cook until the leeks have softened, 4 minutes longer. Taste and season generously with salt and black pepper.

Add the stock and soy sauce and bring the mixture to a boil. Once the soup is rapidly boiling, reduce the heat level to medium and add the chicken, carrots, and udon. Cover and cook for about 10 minutes.

Remove the broth from the heat and stir in the kale. Season once more with salt and pepper. Before serving, I suggest drizzling each individual serving with a tiny (⅛ of a teaspoon) drizzle of sesame oil and topping with a few chile slices, if using.

MAKE-AHEAD TIP *Gingery healing broth can be stored in the fridge for up to 1 week.*

CAN I FREEZE IT? *Gingery healing broth can be stored in the freezer for up to 1 month. Thaw in the fridge overnight or on the counter for a few hours*

HOW TO REHEAT *Transfer to a pot and simmer over medium heat until desired temperature is achieved.*

MAKES 6–8 SERVINGS

This recipe is no-fail, quick, and easy. The combination of ginger and orange marries beautifully with the veal chops—without overpowering or masking their natural taste. Be sure to preheat your grill so it is hot enough to leave those beautiful, golden grill marks on the chops.

GRILLED VEAL CHOPS WITH GRAINY DIJON, GINGER & ORANGE

1	orange, cut in half horizontally
2	tablespoons whole-grain Dijon mustard
2	tablespoons balsamic vinegar
1½	tablespoons extra-virgin olive oil
1	teaspoon whole mustard seeds
1	teaspoon dried rosemary
1	teaspoon kosher salt
½	teaspoon freshly ground black pepper
4–6	thick-cut veal chops (about 1½ inches/4 cm thick)

Grab a medium glass jar and squeeze the orange juice into the jar. Use your fingertips to pull at some of the loose orange flesh and add it to the jar as well. Add the mustard, vinegar, oil, mustard seed, rosemary, and seasonings into the jar. Close the lid tightly and shake well until combined.

Place the veal chops in a large lock-top plastic bag (2 chops per bag, so 2 or 3 bags depending on how many chops you are preparing). Divide the marinade equally and pour over the chops. Seal the bags closed and swoosh the chops around in the bag to coat them with the marinade. Store the bags in the fridge for as little as 10 minutes and up to 48 hours.

Preheat the oven to 425°F (220°C).

Heat a grill pan over medium-high heat. Using metal tongs, remove the chops from the marinade and place on the hot grill pan. Grill, turning once, for 4 minutes per side. Pour the remaining marinade from the plastic bags into a large baking dish that will fit the veal chops. Remove the chops from the pan and place them in the marinade in the baking dish. If serving right away, cover with foil and bake in the oven to your desired doneness: about 3 minutes for medium-rare, 4 minutes for medium, 7 minutes for medium-well.

MAKE-AHEAD TIP *Veal chops may be marinated for up to 48 hours in the fridge until ready to grill. Cooked veal chops may be kept in the fridge for 3 or 4 days. If you are preparing the veal chops in advance and would like to finish cooking them just before serving to avoid over-drying, simply skip the oven cooking at this time. Before serving, preheat the oven to 425°F (220°C) and cook, covered, based on the above doneness levels.*

CAN I FREEZE IT? *Raw veal chops may be frozen in the marinade for up to 3 months. Cooked veal chops and marinade may be frozen for up to 1 month.*

HOW TO REHEAT *Cooked veal chops may be reheated, covered, in a 325°F (165°C) oven for 10 minutes.*

MAKES 4–6 VEAL CHOPS

A Denver steak, or Denver cut, is a very tender cut of beef taken from the chuck or shoulder area of beef cattle. Denver steaks are typically about ¾ inch (2 cm) thick with rich, fat marbling, making them perfect for cooking quickly on the grill and slicing. This cut of meat has become popular in recent years, but if you can't find it, this recipe will work well with beef fillet split (London broil) as well. See my tips below for precooking the steak in advance and reheating.

SLICED DENVER STEAK WITH BALSAMIC VINEGAR & MUSTARD SEEDS

1   teaspoon whole-grain
    Dijon mustard

½   teaspoon Roasted Garlic
    Paste (page 29) or 1 small
    clove garlic, minced

1   tablespoon Worcestershire sauce

1   tablespoon balsamic vinegar

1   teaspoon extra-virgin olive oil

1   teaspoon whole
    mustard seeds

½   teaspoon kosher salt

½   teaspoon dry oregano

¼   teaspoon dried mint

¼   teaspoon freshly ground
    black pepper

2   Denver steaks, ¾ lb (340 g) *each*

In a small bowl, whisk together the mustard, garlic paste, Worcestershire sauce, vinegar, oil, spices, herbs, and seasoning. Place the steak in a large lock-top plastic bag or lidded container. Pour half of the marinade over and press the spices into the steak. Reserve the rest of the marinade for later. Marinate on the counter for 10 minutes (or up to 24 hours in the fridge).

Preheat a grill or grill pan to medium-high heat. Grill the steak until medium-rare, turning once, 4 minutes per side. (If you prefer your steak cooked further, simply transfer the slices to an oven-safe dish and cook, uncovered, in a 375°F [190°C] oven for no more than 5 minutes.) Transfer to a cutting board and let the meat rest for 5 minutes.

Use a chef's knife to slice the steaks against the grain into ¾-inch (2-cm) slices. Spoon the reserved marinade over the slices and serve.

MAKE-AHEAD TIP *The steak can be marinated for up to 24 hours before grilling. Grilled and sliced steak can be cooled and stored in the fridge for up to 2 days. If you're making the steaks ahead of time and planning on reheating them, I suggest undercooking them on the grill (3 minutes per side), so that the meat will not overcook when you reheat it later. See reheating instructions below.*

CAN I FREEZE IT? *Grilled and sliced steak can be stored in an airtight container in the freezer for up to 1 month. Thaw in the fridge overnight.*

HOW TO REHEAT *Let the steak come to room temperature before reheating, uncovered, in a 375°F (190°C) oven for 5–7 minutes.*

MAKES 4–6 SERVINGS

"Kefta" is just another way of saying "ground seasoned beef," but I think it is more than a meatball. It boasts bold flavors and more bite than a typical meatball because I've included pine nuts in the meatball mixture, which combines ground beef and lamb. Using grated potato in place of bread crumbs is a trick I learned from my mom. The potato absorbs the liquid in the meat mixture and results in a very moist kefta. You can use grated potato in any meatball-type recipe.

KEFTA BEEF & LAMB KABOBS WITH LEMONY TAHINI SAUCE

FOR THE KEFTAS

- 1 lb (500 g) ground beef
- ½ lb (250 g) ground lamb
- 1 small onion, minced
- 1 small Yukon Gold potato, peeled and grated finely
- 2 tablespoons toasted pine nuts
- 1 tablespoon chopped fresh flat-leaf parsley
- 1 tablespoon chopped fresh mint
- ½ teaspoon cumin
- ½ teaspoon garlic powder
- ½ teaspoon paprika
  Kosher salt and freshly grated black pepper
  Extra-virgin olive oil

FOR THE LEMONY TAHINI SAUCE

- ½ cup (120 ml) raw tahini
- ½ cup (120 ml) cold water
- ½ teaspoon minced garlic
  Juice of ½ lemon

Preheat the oven to 400°F (200°C). Line a rimmed baking sheet with parchment paper.

To prepare the keftas, in a large bowl, combine the beef, lamb, onion, potato, pine nuts, parsley, mint, cumin, garlic powder, paprika, 1 teaspoon salt, and ½ teaspoon pepper. Use your hands to combine well. To form the keftas, lightly oil your hands with olive oil and take 2 tablespoons of the meat mixture for each kefta. Roll between the palms of your hands, forming an oval-shaped ball (think long rather than fat and round). Place the keftas on the prepared baking sheet, and continue until you have used up all of the meat mixture.

Heat a grill pan over medium-high heat. Grill the keftas for 1–2 minutes per side, and use tongs to transfer them to the parchment-lined baking sheet. Continue cooking in the oven, 5 minutes for medium and 7 minutes for well done.

To prepare the tahini sauce, in a glass jar with a tight-fitting lid, combine the raw tahini, water, garlic, lemon juice, ¼ teaspoon salt, and ¼ teaspoon pepper and shake well until blended. Transfer to a dipping bowl and drizzle with good olive oil. Serve the keftas with the tahini sauce for dipping.

MAKE-AHEAD TIP *Once the meat mixture is combined, you can store it in the fridge for up to 2 days until ready to form and cook the keftas, or you can form the keftas right away. The formed keftas can also be stored in the fridge for up to 2 days before cooking. The tahini sauce can be made up to 4 days in advance, but may need additional water for a thinner consistency. The longer it stays in the fridge, the thicker it will become.*

CAN I FREEZE IT? *The keftas can be frozen for up to 2 months, either before or after cooking. Do not freeze the tahini sauce.*

HOW TO REHEAT *Reheat, covered, in a 300°F (150°C) oven for 10 minutes.*

MAKES 6 SERVINGS

I grew up eating Shake 'n Bake Chicken. I have vivid memories of helping my mom shake the chicken in the bright orange bag of crumbs—it was so easy and fun. And it still is today, though the flavors are more modern. I use the same method in this recipe, but I've added zesty Green Pesto (page 27) to panko (Japanese-style bread crumbs), which results in light, crispy crumbed chicken. This is a family favorite—a recipe you'll bookmark in your mind and make time and time again.

PESTO PANKO CRISPY CHICKEN

6   **chicken legs, skin on and bone in**

6   **chicken thighs, skin on and bone in**

Kosher salt and freshly ground black pepper

1   **cup (100 g) panko**

¼   **cup (60 ml) Green Pesto (page 27)**

1   **tablespoon extra-virgin olive oil**

Preheat the oven to 375°F (190°C). Line a rimmed baking sheet with parchment paper.

Pat the chicken dry using paper towels. Season all the chicken pieces well with salt and pepper and place them on the prepared baking sheet. In a mini food processor, blitz together the panko and pesto. Pulse until the panko is light green and flaky, about 30 seconds or so.

Pour the panko mixture into a large lock-top plastic bag and add 2 pieces of chicken to the bag. Seal the bag and shake it so that the chicken pieces are completely coated with the crumbs. Use tongs to remove the chicken pieces from the bag and place them back on the prepared baking sheet. Repeat with the remaining pieces of chicken.

Arrange all the panko-coated chicken pieces neatly on the baking sheet and drizzle the oil over the top. Bake in the oven, uncovered, until golden and crisp, 45–55 minutes.

MAKE-AHEAD TIP *Pesto panko crispy chicken can be coated up to 24 hours in advance and stored in the fridge, covered, until ready to bake. Cooked chicken may be stored in the fridge for up to 4 days.*

CAN I FREEZE IT? *The chicken can be cooked and stored in the freezer for up to 1 month. Thaw in the fridge overnight.*

HOW TO REHEAT *Reheat, uncovered, in a 350°F (180°C) oven for 10–15 minutes.*

MAKES 6 SERVINGS

This is my go-to recipe for lamb chops. The flavors are bold, but unlike some strong flavor combinations, they don't mask the taste of the lamb—they enhance it. I know that not everyone eats lamb, but everyone loves this rub—so if lamb isn't your choice of meat, try it on chicken or beef. See my tips below for precooking the lamb in advance and reheating.

RED-RUBBED BABY LAMB CHOPS

10 small lamb rib chops, frenched
    Kosher salt and freshly ground
    black pepper
1   tablespoon extra-virgin
    olive oil
1   tablespoon red wine vinegar
    Zest of ½ lemon
½   teaspoon Roasted Garlic
    Paste (page 29) or 1 small
    clove garlic, minced
1   tablespoon paprika
1   teaspoon cumin
1   teaspoon dried rosemary,
    crumbled between your fingers

Lay the chops out on a large piece of parchment paper. Sprinkle both sides of the chops with ½ teaspoon salt and ¼ teaspoon pepper. In a small bowl, whisk together the oil, vinegar, lemon zest, garlic paste, paprika, cumin, and rosemary. Spoon the mixture evenly over the chops and use your fingers to rub it in on both sides.

Preheat a grill or grill pan to medium-high heat. Working in batches if necessary, add the chops and sear for about 2 minutes on the first side. Flip the chops over and cook for another 3 minutes for medium-rare and 3½ minutes for medium. (If you prefer your lamb cooked medium-well, simply transfer the chops to an oven-safe dish and cook, uncovered, in a 375°F [190°C] oven for an additional 3–5 minutes. Save this step until just before serving if you are working ahead.)

Remove from the heat and serve.

MAKE-AHEAD TIP *Red-rubbed baby lamb chops can be cooled and stored in the fridge for up to 2 days. If you're making ahead of time and planning on reheating the lamb, I suggest undercooking it on the grill (2 minutes per side for medium-rare, 2½ minutes for medium), so that the lamb will not overcook when you reheat it later. See reheating instructions below.*

CAN I FREEZE IT? *The lamb chops can be stored in an airtight container in the freezer for up to 1 month. Thaw in the fridge overnight.*

HOW TO REHEAT *Let the lamb come to room temperature before reheating, covered, in a 350°F (180°C) oven for 5–7 minutes.*

MAKES 10 BABY LAMB CHOPS

My son once sat at the dinner table and blurted out: "Turkey burgers are always the same—no matter where you are!" I'm still not sure what prompted the comment (I was in fact serving turkey burgers), but at that moment I made it my mission to prove him wrong. This recipe is the amazing result.

TURKEY SLIDERS WITH SESAME ONIONS

2 **lb (1 kg) ground turkey (I use a blend of white and dark meat)**

1 **large egg**

1 **tablespoon soy sauce**

2 **teaspoons toasted sesame oil**

1 **teaspoon onion powder**

1 **teaspoon garlic powder**

1 **tablespoon sesame seeds**

   Kosher salt and freshly ground black pepper

1 **tablespoon toasted sesame oil**

FOR THE SESAME ONIONS

1 **tablespoon toasted sesame oil**

1 **large yellow onion, thinly sliced**

2 **teaspoons sesame seeds**

   Kosher salt and freshly ground black pepper

In a large bowl, combine the turkey, egg, soy sauce, sesame oil, onion powder, garlic powder, sesame seeds, 1 teaspoon salt, and ½ teaspoon pepper. Use your hands to incorporate all the ingredients into a loose mixture. (I prefer not to add bread crumbs because they tend to dry out my sliders.) If you have time, cover the bowl with plastic wrap and place in the fridge for 1 hour or up to overnight. If you're short on time, cover the bowl and place the mixture in the freezer for 10–15 minutes to firm up.

Remove the bowl from the fridge or freezer and use wet hands to form the mixture into small patties, about ¼ cup (40 g) each. You can also use a regular ice-cream scoop to form equal-size patties. Place a nonstick pan over medium-high heat. Drizzle the sesame oil into the pan and, when it heats up, add the patties. Cook, turning once, until golden brown, about 3 minutes per side.

Cover the pan and reduce the heat to medium. Cook until firm, 8–10 minutes longer. Uncover and remove from the heat. Once they've cooled down a little, transfer the sliders to a serving dish.

To prepare the sesame onions, return the same pan to medium-high heat and add the sesame oil. Add the sliced onion and sauté until caramelized, 6–8 minutes. Stir in the sesame seeds and season with salt and pepper. Remove from the heat and spoon over the burgers. Serve.

MAKE-AHEAD TIP *Turkey sliders with sesame onions can be cooked and stored in the fridge for up to 3 days.*

CAN I FREEZE IT? *The sliders and the onions can be frozen separately or together for up to 1 month. Thaw in the fridge overnight or on the counter for 2 hours.*

HOW TO REHEAT *Reheat, covered, in a 350°F (180°C) oven for 15–20 minutes.*

MAKES 12 TURKEY SLIDERS

It doesn't get easier than this! You know if it says "4 ingredients" in the recipe title, you're going to want to try it! In my opinion, fish should always be served simply. This recipe does the trick. Lemon, ginger, and dill bring out the freshness in each bite without overpowering the flavor of this mild fish.

4-INGREDIENT ARCTIC CHAR

1   **fillet Arctic char, about 2 lb (900 g), skin on**
    Kosher salt and freshly ground black pepper
½   **teaspoon grated ginger**
1   **lemon**
1   **handful of fresh dill**

Preheat the oven to 400°F (200°C). Line a rimmed baking sheet with parchment paper.

Rinse the fish under cold water and pat dry using paper towels. Place the fish skin-side down on the prepared baking sheet. Season the fish with ½ teaspoon salt and ¼ teaspoon pepper. Rub the ginger into the flesh (pink part) of the fish. Cut the lemon in half and squeeze both halves over the fish. Do not discard the lemons. Slice the squeezed-out lemons into the thinnest possible slices that you can. Line the top of the fish with the lemon slices in any decorative fashion that you choose. Roughly chop the dill and sprinkle over the top.

Bake the fish in the oven, uncovered, for 15 minutes. Remove from the heat and serve.

MAKE-AHEAD TIP *The Arctic char can be prepared and stored in the fridge, covered with plastic wrap, for up to 8 hours before cooking.*

HOW TO REHEAT *Do not reheat. If not serving right away, leave the cooked fish at room temperature for up to 2 hours until ready to serve.*

MAKES 4–6 SERVINGS

ONE-PAN MEALS

This recipe epitomizes home cooking for me. I grew up eating a similar dish of *"boulettes et haricots"* (meatballs and string beans), and I can recall dipping pieces of challah into the hot, delicious tomato sauce and scooping up the beans. I've added grated onion and potato to the meat mixture to add great moisture and mild flavors. This recipe can easily be made with ground beef, veal, or even ground lamb.

CHICKEN MEATBALLS WITH STRING BEANS IN TOMATO SAUCE

2   lb (1 kg) ground chicken (I use a blend of dark and white meat)

1   Yukon Gold potato, peeled and grated

1   yellow onion, grated and drained of excess liquid

1   large egg

¼   cup (60 ml) ketchup

1   teaspoon Worcestershire sauce

½   teaspoon onion powder

½   teaspoon ground thyme

½   cup (50 g) seasoned bread crumbs

     Kosher salt and freshly ground black pepper

1   tablespoon light olive oil

½   lb (250 g) string beans, trimmed

1   cup (250 ml) marinara sauce

½   cup (120 ml) chicken stock or water

Combine the chicken, potato, onion, egg, ketchup, Worcestershire sauce, onion powder, thyme, bread crumbs, ½ teaspoon salt, and ¼ teaspoon pepper in a large bowl and use your hands to mix well. Use wet hands to form the mixture into meatballs, about 2 tablespoons each.

In a large sauté pan, heat the oil over medium-high heat. Add the meatballs in a neat, single layer and cook for 3 minutes. Use tongs to flip the meatballs over, starting with the first meatballs you placed in the pan. Once all the meatballs have been flipped over, add the string beans to the pan, placing them directly over the meatballs. Pour the marinara sauce and the stock over the string beans. Raise the temperature to high and bring to a boil. Once the sauce is bubbling, reduce the heat to medium-low and cover. Cook, covered, for 15 minutes. Uncover the pan, spoon some of the sauce over the string beans, and raise the heat to medium-high. Cook for 5 minutes longer to thicken the sauce. Serve.

MAKE-AHEAD TIP *The meatball mixture can be formed and stored in the fridge for up to 1 day before cooking. Chicken meatballs with string beans in tomato sauce can be stored in an airtight container in the fridge for up to 3 days.*

CAN I FREEZE IT? *The meatball mixture can be formed and stored in the freezer for up to 2 months.*

HOW TO REHEAT *Bring chicken meatballs with string beans in tomato sauce to room temperature before reheating, covered, on the stove top over medium heat for 5 minutes or in the oven at 350°F (180°C) for 5–7 minutes.*

MAKES 4–6 SERVINGS

ONE-PAN
MEALS

I am not sure how chicken drumsticks morphed into "kiddie food," but it seems that they have. Whenever I am having company with kids over for a meal, I make this dish for the younger set. It's a no-brainer—sweet, sticky, and yum, with your veggies and protein all in one big baking dish.

SESAME CHICKEN DRUMSTICKS WITH CRISPY BROCCOLI & BROCCOLINI

12 **chicken legs, trimmed of excess skin and fat**

1 **cup (250 ml) Toasted Sesame Marinade (page 33)**

1 **head broccoli, cut into florets**

1 **head broccolini, cut into florets**

1 **tablespoon sesame seeds**

Preheat the oven to 350°F (180°C).

Place the chicken in a large baking dish. Pour the marinade over the chicken and turn to coat all the pieces in the sauce. Place each of the broccoli florets in each of the 4 corners of the baking dish, and scatter the broccolini around the chicken pieces. Cover with foil and bake for 30 minutes.

Remove from the oven and uncover, and sprinkle the sesame seeds over the top. Raise the oven temperature to 375°F (190°C) and bake for 20 minutes longer. Remove from the oven and serve.

MAKE-AHEAD TIP *Sesame chicken drumsticks can be marinated and stored in the fridge for up to 24 hours before cooking. Add the broccoli and broccolini just before cooking.*

HOW TO REHEAT *Let the chicken come to room temperature before reheating, uncovered, in a 350°F (180°C) oven for 7–10 minutes.*

MAKES 4–6 SERVINGS

Chicken, rice, and sweet potato slices, roasted together in the oven, release juices and flavors that will make your mouth water. I know that most people might not opt for rice *and* potatoes in the same sitting, but I love the contrast of the soft, buttery sweet potato slices against the bright lemons and crunchy rice. If you'd rather skip the potatoes, go ahead . . . but I'm warning you that the experience just won't be the same! You can use chicken pieces, skin on and bone in, for the butterflied chicken.

CRISPY CHICKEN WITH RICE, SWEET POTATOES & LEMON SLICES

FOR THE CHICKEN

Extra-virgin olive oil

2 sweet potatoes, scrubbed, trimmed, and cut into ⅛-inch (3-mm) slices

1 large yellow onion, cut into ⅛-inch (3-mm) slices

Kosher salt and freshly ground black pepper

1 lemon (preferably Meyer), scrubbed and cut into ⅛-inch (3-mm) slices

Juice of 1 lemon

1 tablespoon Worcestershire sauce

1 teaspoon onion powder

4 sprigs thyme or 1 teaspoon dried thyme

1 whole butterflied chicken, skin on and bone in, trimmed of excess skin and fat

FOR THE RICE

1 cup (200 g) long-grain white rice

1 teaspoon light olive oil

½ teaspoon turmeric

Zest of 1 lemon

Kosher salt and freshly ground black pepper

2 cups (500 ml) boiling water

Preheat the oven to 375°F (190°C).

To prepare the chicken, drizzle 1 tablespoon extra-virgin olive oil into a large baking dish (at least 9 by 12 inches/23 by 30 cm). Add the sweet potato and onion slices, season with salt and pepper, and toss them in the oil. Arrange the potato and onion slices in a single layer in the base of the dish. Place the lemon slices over them.

In a small bowl, whisk together the lemon juice, Worcestershire sauce, onion powder, and thyme. Drizzle this mixture all over the chicken and rub into the top and underside of the chicken, coating it as much as you can. Place the seasoned chicken, skin side up, in the center of the baking dish.

To prepare the rice, rinse the rice under cold running water and drain. Transfer to a small bowl and stir in the light olive oil, turmeric, lemon zest, ½ teaspoon salt, and ¼ teaspoon pepper. Scatter the rice around the chicken in the baking dish. Pour the boiling water directly over the scattered rice (but not over the chicken). Cover the dish tightly with aluminum foil and bake in the oven for 45 minutes. Remove from the oven and uncover. Return to the oven to cook until crispy, 30 minutes longer.

MAKE-AHEAD TIP *Crispy chicken and rice with sweet potato and lemon slices (without the rice) can be marinated and stored in the fridge for up to 24 hours. Add the seasoned rice and boiling water just before cooking.*

HOW TO REHEAT *Crispy chicken and rice with sweet potato and lemon slices can be reheated, uncovered, in a 350°F (180°C) oven for 10 minutes.*

MAKES 4–6 SERVINGS

Herbes de Provence is a dried herb blend typically used in the Provence region of southern France. The blend usually includes savory, marjoram, thyme, oregano, and lavender. Herbes de Provence is readily available at most grocery stores, but you can also mix your own. This recipe follows the basic method for my crispy chicken and rice recipe (page 110). It is a one-pan sensation—golden roasted chicken surrounded by crispy rice infused with chicken flavors and seasonings. I've yet to have a single grain of rice left over from this dish!

HERBES DE PROVENCE & ROSEMARY ROASTED CHICKEN WITH CRISPY RICE

FOR THE CHICKEN

- 1 **whole butterflied chicken, skin on and bone in, trimmed of excess skin and fat**
- 1 **tablespoon extra-virgin olive oil**
- 2 **teaspoons Roasted Garlic Paste (page 29) or 3 cloves garlic, minced**
- 3 **tablespoons herbes de Provence**
- 1 **tablespoon dried rosemary, crushed between your fingers**
- ½ **teaspoon garlic powder**
  Kosher salt and freshly ground black pepper

FOR THE RICE

- 1 **cup (200 g) long-grain white rice**
- 1 **teaspoon light olive oil**
- ½ **teaspoon turmeric**
  Kosher salt and freshly ground black pepper
- 2 **cups (500 ml) boiling water**

Preheat the oven to 375°F (190°C).

To prepare the chicken, lay the bird out flat, skin side up, in a large baking dish (at least 9 by 12 inches/23 by 30 cm). Drizzle the extra-virgin olive oil over the top of the chicken. Sprinkle the garlic paste, herbes de Provence, rosemary, garlic powder, 1 teaspoon salt, and ½ teaspoon pepper all over the chicken and rub the flavorings into the top and underside of the chicken, coating it as much as you can.

To prepare the rice, rinse the rice under cold running water and drain. Transfer to a small bowl and stir in the light olive oil, turmeric, ½ teaspoon salt, and ¼ teaspoon pepper. Scatter the rice around the chicken in the baking dish. Pour the boiling water directly over the scattered rice (but not over the chicken). Cover the dish tightly with aluminum foil and bake in the oven for 45 minutes. Remove from the oven and uncover. Return to the oven to cook until crispy, 30 minutes longer. Let cool for a few minutes before serving directly from the baking dish.

MAKE-AHEAD TIP *Herbes de Provence and rosemary roasted chicken (without the rice) can be marinated and stored in the fridge for up to 24 hours. Add the seasoned rice and boiling water just before cooking.*

HOW TO REHEAT *Herbes de Provence and rosemary roasted chicken with crispy rice can be reheated, uncovered, in a 350°F (180°C) oven for 10 minutes.*

MAKES 4–6 SERVINGS

Sumac, a spice commonly used in the Middle East, has a tart flavor that is reminiscent of vinegar or lemon, and a rusty, purple color. Sumac can be purchased online or at specialty grocers (unless you live in New York City, where your corner bodega probably carries sumac!). I love mixing the sweet roasted red onions with the tart sumac and sweet honey. The flavors, when combined, are so wonderful and complex that not much more is needed. I've suggested making it with a whole chicken cut into eight pieces, but if you have a preference for dark or white meat, feel free to switch it up to breasts or thighs only.

ROASTED CHICKEN, RED ONIONS, SUMAC & HONEY

1   chicken, cut into 8 pieces, skin on and bone in, trimmed of excess skin and fat

3   red onions, peeled and cut into 8 wedges

2   tablespoons light olive oil

2   tablespoons balsamic vinegar
    Kosher salt and freshly ground black pepper

1   tablespoon sumac

¼   cup (60 ml) honey

Preheat the oven to 400°F (200°C). Line a rimmed baking sheet with parchment paper.

Arrange the chicken and onions on the prepared baking sheet. Drizzle the oil and vinegar over the chicken and onions and toss well. Sprinkle with ¾ teaspoon salt, ¼ teaspoon pepper, and the sumac, and toss all together. Bake in the oven, uncovered, for 45 minutes. Remove from the oven, drizzle the honey over the top, and return to the oven until golden, 20 minutes longer.

MAKE-AHEAD TIP *Roasted chicken, red onions, sumac, and honey can be assembled and marinated in the fridge for up to 24 hours before cooking. If marinating, do not add the sumac until just before cooking. Sumac can turn your chicken purple when marinated.*

HOW TO REHEAT *Let the chicken come to room temperature before reheating, uncovered, in a 350°F (180°C) oven for 7–10 minutes.*

MAKES 4–6 SERVINGS

As my kids get older, I've noticed that roasting one chicken for dinner is simply not enough. So, these days, it's two chickens and lots of potatoes for my family. This recipe is simple, easy, and the kids love it. "Hasselback" is a term for potatoes sliced very thin, but with the bottoms left intact, so the thin slices fan out and can easily be peeled off, one slice at a time. The potatoes, alongside the beautiful golden roasted chickens, are best served hot, right out of the oven.

SIMPLE ROASTED CHICKENS WITH HASSELBACK POTATOES

FOR THE CHICKEN

- **2** whole butterflied chickens, skin on and bone in, trimmed of excess skin and fat
  Kosher salt and freshly ground black pepper
- **2** lemons, halved
- **2** tablespoons extra-virgin olive oil
- **2** teaspoons Roasted Garlic Paste (page 29) or 2 teaspoons minced fresh garlic
- **4** sprigs fresh thyme, thyme leaves plucked off the stem or 1 teaspoon dried thyme

FOR THE HASSELBACK POTATOES

- **6–10** medium to large Yukon Gold potatoes, scrubbed and dried
  Light olive oil
  Kosher salt and freshly ground black pepper

Preheat the oven to 375°F (190°C). Line an extra-large rimmed baking sheet (or 2 regular baking sheets) with parchment paper.

To prepare the chickens, season them with salt and pepper on both sides—be generous! Squeeze the lemons over the chickens, then drizzle with the extra-virgin olive oil. Rub the garlic paste and thyme on both sides of the chickens. Place the chickens, skin side up, on the prepared baking sheet.

To prepare the Hasselback potatoes, working with one potato at a time, cut thin slits into the top of the potato from one side to the other, cutting almost but not all the way through, almost like a fan. Drizzle the light olive oil over the potatoes and season generously with salt and pepper, then use your hands to rub in the seasonings and ensure that the potatoes are completely coated with the oil, salt, and pepper. Place the potatoes, uncut side down, around the chickens on the same baking sheet.

Cover the baking sheet with aluminum foil and bake in the oven for 45 minutes. Uncover and bake until both the chickens and potatoes are crispy and golden, 30 minutes longer. Serve.

MAKE-AHEAD TIP *The chickens can be marinated and stored in the fridge for up to 24 hours before cooking. Cooked chickens with potatoes can be stored in an airtight container in the fridge for up to 4 days.*

HOW TO REHEAT *The chickens with potatoes can be reheated, uncovered, in a 350°F (180°C) oven for 10 minutes.*

MAKES 6–10 SERVINGS

This is a quick-and-easy dinner that can be ready in no time flat. Chicken thighs are wonderful when cooked alongside bright vegetables, because they can stand the heat without drying out. The combination of earthy carrots, cherry tomatoes, and green pesto is a winning one. To serve, I like to transfer the chicken and vegetables to a large platter and top with an aromatic bunch of fresh basil and some extra back pepper.

CHICKEN THIGHS WITH ROASTED CARROTS & CHERRY TOMATOES

12 skinless, boneless chicken thighs

1 yellow onion, cut into thin slices

6 medium carrots, stemmed and cut into quarters lengthwise

2 cups (360 g) assorted cherry tomatoes

Kosher salt and freshly ground black pepper

¾ cup (180 ml) Green Pesto (page 27)

1 tablespoon extra-virgin olive oil

Fresh basil leaves for garnish

Preheat the oven to 375°F (190°C). Line a rimmed baking sheet with parchment paper.

Place the chicken, onions, carrots, and tomatoes on the prepared baking sheet. Season with ¾ teaspoon salt and ½ teaspoon pepper. Drizzle the pesto over all of the ingredients and use your hands to rub it into the chicken and veggies. Pat the chicken and veggies down so they are in a single layer on the parchment paper. Drizzle the oil over the top. Bake in the oven, uncovered, for 45 minutes. Transfer to a serving dish and top with fresh basil and some extra pepper.

MAKE-AHEAD TIP *Chicken thighs with roasted carrots and cherry tomatoes can be assembled and marinated in the fridge for up to 24 hours. Bring to room temperature before cooking.*

CAN I FREEZE IT? *Chicken thighs can be stored in the freezer for up to 1 month. Thaw in the fridge overnight.*

HOW TO REHEAT *Let the chicken come to room temperature before reheating, uncovered, in a 350°F (180°C) oven for 7–10 minutes.*

MAKES 4–6 SERVINGS

Whenever I serve this recipe, I serve it directly from the baking sheet it is cooked on. Usually it's on Sunday night in front of a TV blaring a football game. The spicy peanut sauce spiked with fresh lime juice is a huge hit, so much so that I don't even think the guys realize that the crispy little bits they're dipping into it are brussels sprouts!

CHICKEN STRIPS & CRUNCHY BRUSSELS SPROUTS WITH SPICY PEANUT SIP

6 **skinless, boneless chicken breast halves, cut into 1-inch (2.5-cm) strips (do not use pounded, thin cutlets)**
   Kosher salt and freshly ground black pepper

1 **batch Spicy Peanut Sip (page 32)**

1 **lb (500 g) brussels sprouts, cut into quarters**

2 **tablespoons extra-virgin olive oil**

½ **teaspoon onion powder**
   Juice of 2 limes

Preheat the oven to 375°F (190°C). Line a rimmed baking sheet with parchment paper.

Place the chicken in a medium bowl, season with salt and pepper, and add ½ cup (120 ml) of the peanut sip. Toss and set aside.

In a large bowl, toss together the brussels sprouts, oil, and onion powder. Tip the brussels sprouts into the center of the pan. Place the chicken strips on the edge of the pan, framing the brussels sprouts. (Discard the marinade.) Bake in the oven until the chicken is sizzling and the brussels sprouts are golden, 20–25 minutes.

Add the lime juice to the remaining peanut sip. Serve with the chicken and brussels sprouts for dipping.

MAKE-AHEAD TIP *Chicken strips can be marinated in peanut sauce and stored in the fridge for up to 48 hours. Cook as indicated in the recipe above.*

HOW TO REHEAT *Let the chicken come to room temperature before reheating, uncovered, in a 350°F (180°C) oven for 7–10 minutes.*

MAKES 4–6 SERVINGS

YOU CAN ENTERTAIN, FEED
FAMILY AND FRIENDS, OR HAVE
AN INTIMATE EVERYDAY MEAL
WITH STYLE AND INSPIRATION
WHILE ACTUALLY ENJOYING
YOURSELF. AND YOU SHOULD.

Simply braised halibut served over a bed of chopped chickpeas, herbs, and spices can be ready in under twenty minutes and is a perfect, healthy choice for lunch or dinner. I love that this recipe can equally satisfy toddlers, schoolchildren, or adults with sophisticated palates. Swap out the halibut for your favorite fish and experiment with different veggies, like cherry tomatoes and zucchini, to make this dish your own.

HALIBUT WITH BLITZED CHICKPEAS, CARROTS, LEMON & GARLIC

3 carrots, peeled and cut into chunks

1 red bell pepper, stemmed and seeded, cut into chunks

¼ of a lemon, skin on, seeds removed, cut into small chunks

2 cloves garlic

2 tablespoons chopped cilantro or Herb Chop Chop (page 33)

1 can (15 oz/430 g) chickpeas, drained and rinsed

1 tablespoon light olive oil

1 teaspoon turmeric

1 tablespoon paprika

Kosher salt and freshly ground black pepper

6 skinless halibut fillets, about 6 oz (180 g) each

Extra-virgin olive oil

In a food processor, combine the carrots, bell pepper, lemon, and garlic. Process until chopped into small pieces. Add the cilantro and chickpeas and pulse 1 or 2 times until all the ingredients are chopped into tiny pieces, but not mushy.

In a large sauté pan, heat the light olive oil over medium-high heat. Add the chickpea mixture and stir in the turmeric and paprika. Season generously with salt and pepper to taste. Cook the mixture until bubbly, about 3 minutes.

Reduce the heat to medium-low. Season the halibut with salt and pepper, and place the fish in the chickpea mixture. Drizzle the halibut with extra-virgin olive oil, cover, and simmer for 10 minutes. Uncover and spoon some of the sauce and chickpea mixture over the fish before serving.

MAKE-AHEAD TIP *The chickpea mixture can be prepared up to 2 days in advance and stored in an airtight container in the fridge. Halibut with blitzed chickpeas, carrots, lemon, and garlic can be prepared up to 4 hours in advance and stored in the fridge.*

HOW TO REHEAT *Halibut with blitzed chickpeas, carrots, lemon and garlic can be reheated in a sauté pan, partially covered, over medium heat for about 5 minutes.*

MAKES 4–6 SERVINGS

It's always amazed me how many people are fearful of cooking fish. They worry about overcooking it, undercooking it, the house smelling fishy . . . and the list goes on when, to my mind, there is nothing easier to cook than fish. It is quick and easy, and you don't need to do much to it. In fact, when it comes to fish, less is definitely more. While I know that the thought of preparing an entire fish may seem daunting, let me tell you a secret: Cooking fish whole is probably the most foolproof way to cook fish. It is almost impossible to overcook the fish when you are cooking it whole.

LEMONY WHOLE BRANZINO & POTATOES IN THE OVEN

FOR THE BRANZINO

6   whole branzino, 1 lb (500 g) each, scaled and gutted (ask your fishmonger to do this)
    Kosher salt and freshly ground black pepper

¼   cup (60 ml) extra-virgin olive oil
    Juice of 1 lemon

2   tablespoons capers (optional)

1   lemon, cut into thin slices

6   sprigs fresh rosemary

FOR THE POTATOES

5   Yukon Gold potatoes, peeled and cut into thin (¼-inch/6-mm) slices

¼   cup (60 ml) extra-virgin olive oil

3   cloves garlic, minced
    Juice of 1 lemon
    Kosher salt and freshly ground black pepper

Preheat the oven to 400°F (200°C). Line a rimmed baking sheet with parchment paper.

To prepare the branzino, place the fish on the prepared baking sheet. Season the inside cavities as well as the outside of each fish with salt and pepper. In a small bowl, stir together the oil, lemon juice, and capers, if using. Drizzle the mixture over the inside and outside of each fish. Stuff 1–2 lemon slices and 1 sprig of rosemary inside the cavity of each fish.

To prepare the potatoes, in a large bowl, toss together the sliced potatoes, oil, garlic, lemon juice, 1 teaspoon salt, and ¼ teaspoon pepper. Scatter the seasoned potatoes (and all their marinade) around and in between the fish on the baking sheet.

Roast until potatoes and fish appear crispy, 20–25 minutes.

MAKE-AHEAD TIP *Lemony whole branzino and potatoes can be assembled and stored in the fridge for up to 6 hours. Bring to room temperature before cooking.*

MAKES 6 SERVINGS

This is my healthy version of steak and chips—spice-rubbed salmon steaks baked in the oven surrounded by kale chips that have been flavored with salt and vinegar. As the salmon steaks roast in the oven, the kale chips curl and crisp up alongside. This recipe can be made with any fish steaks or fillets, and the kale chips are best when eaten right out of the oven.

ROASTED SALMON STEAKS WITH SALT & VINEGAR KALE CHIPS

FOR THE SALMON STEAKS

6   salmon steaks, ½ inch (12 mm) thick
     Kosher salt and freshly ground black pepper

1   teaspoon chili powder

¼   teaspoon ground ginger

¼   teaspoon ground cumin

1   teaspoon extra-virgin olive oil

1   tablespoon tomato paste

1   teaspoon white vinegar

FOR THE KALE CHIPS

4   handfuls of Washed & Stored Kale (page 22)

2   tablespoons extra-virgin olive oil

2   tablespoons white vinegar
     Kosher salt and freshly ground black pepper

Preheat the oven to 375°F (190°C). Line a rimmed baking sheet with parchment paper.

To prepare the salmon steaks, place the fish on the prepared baking sheet. Season both sides of the salmon with salt and pepper. In a small bowl, stir together the spices, oil, tomato paste, and vinegar. Brush this mixture over both sides of the salmon, using it all up.

To prepare the kale chips, put the kale in a large bowl and add the oil, vinegar, 1 teaspoon salt, and ½ teaspoon pepper. Toss together so all of the kale pieces are coated.

Scatter the kale around, but not over, the fish on the baking sheet. Bake, uncovered, for 20 minutes. Serve right away.

MAKE-AHEAD TIP *The salmon steaks can be marinated and stored in the fridge for up to 12 hours.*

HOW TO REHEAT *Roasted salmon steaks with salt and vinegar kale chips can be brought to room temperature and reheated, uncovered, in a 350°F (180°C) oven for 5 minutes.*

MAKES 4–6 SERVINGS

When I was a child, my mom would serve us braised leeks drizzled with creamy vinaigrette. Even at a young age, I recall enjoying the buttery sweetness of the leeks. The recipe below is a great combination of those sweet, caramelized leeks and simply braised cod. The cod may be replaced with any fish fillets of your choice. Be sure to wash the leeks thoroughly by soaking them in a big bowl of water as described here, to remove all the grit hiding between its many layers.

CARAMELIZED LEEKS & BRAISED COD

4   **leeks**

2   **tablespoons light olive oil**

½   **teaspoon sugar**

    Kosher salt and freshly ground black pepper

6   **skinless cod fillets, ½ lb (250 g)** *each*

¼   **cup (60 ml) white wine**

3   **saffron threads**

1   **teaspoon fresh lemon juice**

Trim away the dark green tops of the leeks, leaving only the white and light green parts. Halve them lengthwise, leaving the root end intact. Place in a large bowl of water and swish around to remove dirt from the layers.

Heat a large sauté pan over medium-high heat. Add the oil and sprinkle the sugar, ¼ teaspoon salt, and ¼ teaspoon pepper all over the bottom of the pan. Add the leeks in a single layer, cut side down. Cook until golden brown and caramelized, about 5 minutes.

Season the tops of the cod fillets with salt and pepper. Place the cod over the leeks, and pour the wine over the fish. Sprinkle the saffron and lemon juice over the cod. Reduce the heat to low, cover, and simmer for 10–15 minutes. Let rest for a few minutes before serving.

MAKE-AHEAD TIP *Caramelized leeks can be made up to 24 hours ahead and stored in an airtight container in the fridge. Bring to room temperature before returning them to the sauté pan and cooking the fish. Caramelized leeks and braised cod will be best served the day it is made, but can be stored in the fridge in an airtight container for up to 2 days.*

HOW TO REHEAT *Caramelized leeks and braised cod can be reheated on the stove top, covered, over medium heat for 5–7 minutes.*

MAKES 6–8 SERVINGS

A side of salmon can always feed a big crowd, and this recipe—a staple of mine—works well for guests of all ages and palates. Beautiful salmon topped with crunchy spiralized squash and zucchini ribbons: the colors are gorgeous and the taste is delicious. You just can't go wrong. I like my crunchies really crunchy, and in order to crisp them up without burning them, once they've gotten 75 percent as crispy as I want them to be, I turn the oven off and leave them in there overnight.

ROASTED SALMON TOPPED WITH SQUASH & ZUCCHINI CRUNCHIES

FOR THE CRUNCHIES

 2 **cups (230 g) spiralized butternut squash**
 2 **cups (230 g) spiralized zucchini**
 3 **tablespoons melted coconut oil**
    Kosher salt and freshly ground black pepper

FOR THE SALMON

1- to 3-lb (450 g–1.4 kg) side of salmon, skin removed
    Kosher salt and freshly ground black pepper
 1 **teaspoon paprika**
    Sea salt

Preheat the oven to 350°F (180°C). Line 2 rimmed baking sheets with parchment paper.

To prepare the crunchies, in a large bowl, toss together the squash, zucchini, oil, 1 teaspoon salt, and ½ teaspoon pepper. Transfer the squash and zucchini to the prepared baking sheets. Make sure you don't overcrowd the baking sheets. If you need one more sheet, please use it. Bake until crisp, 30–40 minutes, tossing the veggies halfway through baking to prevent burning. Remove from the oven and set aside. If the squash and zucchini aren't as crispy as you'd like them, reduce the oven temperature to 300°F (150°C) and let them bake longer. Check on them every 10 minutes.

To prepare the salmon, preheat the oven to 400°F (200°C). Line a rimmed baking sheet with parchment paper.

Place the fish on the prepared baking sheet and season with salt and pepper. Rub the paprika into the salmon flesh. Bake until golden and firm to the touch, about 10–15 minutes per pound. Transfer the fish to a serving dish. Before serving, scatter the crunchies over the salmon. Sprinkle a little sea salt over the top. The dish may be served hot or at room temperature.

MAKE-AHEAD TIP *The crunchies can be made up to 4 days in advance and stored, uncovered, in a glass Pyrex dish or on baking sheets in a dry place. The salmon can be seasoned and stored in the fridge for up to 24 hours before cooking. After cooking, roasted salmon topped with crunchies can be stored in an airtight container in the fridge for up to 3 days, but will be best on the day it is cooked.*

HOW TO REHEAT *Roasted salmon topped with squash and zucchini crunchies can be reheated, uncovered, in a 300°F (150°C) oven for 10 minutes. Or, serve at room temperature.*

MAKES 6–8 SERVINGS

HOT, SLOW
& SIMMERED

This is my go-to recipe for a lazy winter night. Root vegetables and a whole chicken slowly simmered in a bottle of white wine—my idea of comfort food! Please improvise with the root vegetables of your choice. Serve with a crusty French baguette—you won't even need plates. It's perfect for a romantic dinner (just saying).

A BOTTLE OF WINE & CHICKEN

2   tablespoons light olive oil

2   yellow onions, diced

3   sweet potatoes, peeled
    and cut into quarters

3   Yukon Gold potatoes, peeled
    and cut into quarters

1   fennel bulb, trimmed, cored,
    and cut into quarters

2   yellow beets, trimmed, peeled
    and cut into quarters

    Kosher salt and freshly ground
    black pepper

1   whole chicken, cleaned
    and patted dry

½   teaspoon turmeric

1   bunch fresh sage, tied with
    kitchen string

1   bottle of dry white wine
    (I use Sauvignon Blanc)

In a large Dutch oven or large stove top roasting pot, heat the oil over medium-high heat. Add the diced onions and sauté until light brown, about 10 minutes. Add the sweet potatoes and potatoes, fennel, and beets. Reduce the heat to medium. Use a wooden spoon to toss all of the vegetables together with the onions, about 10 minutes longer. Season generously with salt and pepper.

Place the chicken on a parchment-lined work surface. Season the chicken with salt and pepper, inside and out. Rub the turmeric into the skin. Place the chicken over the veggies.

Pour the entire bottle of wine over the chicken and vegetables. Top the chicken with the sage and bring to a boil. Reduce the heat to medium-low, so it is simmering slowly, and cover. Simmer until the chicken is falling apart, 2 hours. Uncover and cook over medium-high heat for 20 minutes longer to thicken the liquid. Discard the sage, and serve.

MAKE-AHEAD TIP *A bottle of wine and chicken can stay in the pot on the counter for up to 2 hours or in the fridge for up to 3 days.*

HOW TO REHEAT *Over medium heat on the stove top until hot, 10 minutes.*

MAKES 4–6 SERVINGS

Where should I start when it comes to bone broth? A genuine healer, it is filled with rich nutrients that are good for you on so many levels. The longer you cook this nourishing broth, the more savory and concentrated it becomes. Sip this restorative broth on its own, use it as a cooking liquid for grains or veggies, or use it as a base for a soup. My personal favorite is to sip it on its own sprinkled with lots of fresh flat-leaf parsley. This method may seem like a long process, but it's well worth the effort.

BONE MARROW BROTH WITH CIPOLLINI ONIONS & PARSLEY

1   lb (500 g) cipollini onions, peeled and kept whole

4   lb (1.8 kg) beef marrow bones

3   carrots, unpeeled

3   ribs celery, halved

3   tablespoons apple cider vinegar

8–10   cups (2–2.5 L) water

2   bay leaves

1   bunch fresh flat-leaf parsley

2   peppercorns (optional)

Kosher salt and freshly ground black pepper

Preheat the oven to 450°F (230°C).

Place the onions, bones, carrots, and celery on a large, unlined rimmed baking sheet. Place on the center rack of the oven and roast for 20 minutes. Remove from the oven and transfer everything on the baking sheet, including the tiny browned bits and pieces, into a large soup pot (if you have an enameled cast-iron one, use it). Pour the vinegar over and add the water, filling the pot three-fourths of the way. Toss in the bay leaves, parsley, and peppercorns, if using.

Cover the pot and bring to a boil. Reduce the heat to maintain a low simmer and cook, partially covered, occasionally skimming the foam from the top of the pot, for at least 6 or up to 24 hours. (Do not leave on the stove top unattended; remove from the heat, let cool, and continue simmering the next day.) The longer it simmers, the better the broth will be. Add more water if necessary to ensure that bones and vegetables are fully submerged. You can cook the broth in a slow cooker on low for the same amount of time.

Remove from the heat and let cool slightly. Ladle the broth through a fine-mesh strainer. Discard the bones, vegetables, and herbs. Season with salt and pepper.

NOTE *Bone broth made from marrow bones tends to be somewhat oily. After chilling the broth, the fat floats to the top and coagulates, making it easy to scoop away and discard.*

MAKE-AHEAD TIP *Bone marrow broth should be cooled completely before storing in the fridge or freezer. This soup can be stored in the fridge for up to 5 days.*

CAN I FREEZE IT? *Bone marrow broth can be stored in the freezer for up to 6 months. Thaw in the fridge overnight or on the counter for a few hours.*

HOW TO REHEAT *Reheat on the stove top over medium heat for about 10 minutes.*

MAKES ABOUT 2 QT (2 L)

Carrot-ginger meets minestrone in this flavorful, colorful soup medley. Using packaged peeled baby carrots makes this soup easy as can be. (I don't use baby carrots for anything else!) We all know that carrots and ginger are a great match, but here I've added some texture to the recipe: curly pasta, chicken strips, and kale, all for a healthy, satisfying soup.

CARROT-GINGER SOUP WITH CURLY PASTA, KALE & CHICKEN

2	tablespoons light olive oil
3	onions, peeled and thinly sliced
Four	1-lb (500-g) bags peeled baby carrots
One	3-inch (7.5-cm) piece of ginger, peeled and grated, or 2 tablespoons jarred grated ginger
8–10	cups (2–2.5 L) vegetable or chicken stock or water
	Half of a 16-oz/500-g box fusilli pasta
6	skinless, boneless chicken breast halves (do not use thinly pounded ones), cut into strips ½-inch (12 mm) thick
3	handfuls of Washed & Stored Kale (page 22), roughly chopped
	Kosher salt and freshly ground black pepper

In a large pot, heat the oil over medium-high heat. Add the onions and sauté until golden, 10–15 minutes. Add the carrots and ginger and toss with the sautéed onions. Pour the stock over the carrots, filling the pot three-fourths of the way. Bring to a boil. Reduce the heat to medium, cover, and cook until the carrots are tender, about 45 minutes.

Meanwhile, in a separate pot, cook the pasta according to the package directions. Drain and set aside.

Remove the soup from the heat and let cool slightly. Use an immersion blender to purée the mixture until smooth. (Alternatively, transfer the soup to a blender and purée, working in batches.) Return the soup to the pot and bring to a boil. Add the chicken strips and cook, uncovered, until the chicken is cooked through, 10 minutes. Remove from the heat and stir in the pasta and kale. Season generously with salt and pepper. Serve at once.

MAKE-AHEAD TIP *The soup should be cooled completely before storing in the fridge or freezer. The soup can be stored in the fridge for up to 1 week.*

CAN I FREEZE IT? *The soup can be stored in the freezer for up to 2 months. Thaw in the fridge overnight or on the counter for a few hours.*

HOW TO REHEAT *Reheat on the stove top over medium heat for about 10 minutes.*

MAKES ABOUT 10 CUPS (2.4 L)

This is my family's favorite soup. I call it Sunday Soup because I make it every Sunday. It's a full meal in a bowl. Hearty vegetables, juicy chicken, and just the right amount of barley. This versatile soup can be made with any vegetables—there's no need to stick to the recipe below; just use what you have on hand and leave out what you don't. And, don't fret if you don't have chicken or vegetable stock; I've made this soup using water as the liquid many times and it always turns out delicious.

SUNDAY SOUP: VEGGIES, CHICKEN & BARLEY

2   **onions, peeled and cut into chunks**

4   **carrots, peeled and cut into chunks**

    Half of a butternut squash, peeled, seeded, and cut into chunks

1   **zucchini, trimmed and cut into chunks**

1   **sweet potato, peeled and cut into chunks**

2   **tablespoons light olive oil**

8–10   **cups (2–2.5 L) vegetable or chicken stock or water**

6   **skinless, boneless chicken thighs**

1   **bunch fresh dill, tied with kitchen string**

1   **cup (200 g) raw pearl barley Kosher salt and freshly ground black pepper**

Combine all of the vegetables in the workbowl of a food processor. Pulse a few times until all of the vegetables are chopped into tiny pieces, but don't let them get mushy.

In a large pot, heat the oil over medium-high heat. Add the vegetables and sauté for 5 minutes, stirring constantly with a wooden spoon. Cover the pot and reduce the heat to medium. Simmer until the vegetables are soft, 5–7 minutes longer.

Pour the stock or water over the vegetables, filling the pot three-fourths of the way. Stir in the chicken thighs and add the entire bunch of dill (you will fish it out later). Cook, covered, over medium heat for 1 hour.

Use a slotted spoon to fish out the bunch of dill, and discard. Stir in the barley and simmer, covered, until the barley is softened but not mushy, 30–40 minutes longer. Remove the chicken, use a large fork to shred it into small pieces, then return it to the pot. Season generously with salt and pepper. Serve at once.

MAKE-AHEAD TIP *The soup should be cooled completely before storing in the fridge or freezer. This soup can be stored in the fridge for up to 1 week.*

CAN I FREEZE IT? *The soup may be stored in the freezer for up to 2 months. Thaw in the fridge overnight or on the counter for a few hours.*

HOW TO REHEAT *Reheat on the stove top over medium heat for about 10 minutes.*

MAKES ABOUT 10 CUPS (2.5 L)

French roast, also called "brick roast," comes from the top of the chuck and is a flavorful, moist cut—ideal for one-pot cooking. Slow-cooking the meat over a low temperature ensures soft, tender meat and sweet-roasted garlic cloves. I love the contrast of topping the dark roast with a heaping mound of fragrant green basil. It's sure to wow your guests.

TAMARI GARLIC BEEF ROAST WITH FRESH BASIL

1	**French roast or other beef chuck roast, 3–4 lb (1.4–1.8 kg)**
	Kosher salt and freshly ground black pepper
1	**cup (240 ml) tamari**
¼	**cup (60 ml) apple cider vinegar**
2	**tablespoons light olive oil**
1	**can (6 oz/180 g) tomato paste**
¼	**cup (60 ml) honey**
1	**tablespoon dried rosemary**
10	**whole cloves garlic, peeled**
1	**bunch fresh basil, leaves picked**

Season both sides of the roast with salt and pepper. In a medium bowl, whisk together the tamari, vinegar, oil, tomato paste, honey, and rosemary. Place the roast in a large lock-top plastic bag and pour the marinade over it. Add the garlic cloves. Seal the bag and marinate in the fridge for at least 30 minutes or up to 48 hours.

Preheat the oven to 300°F (150°C). Transfer the roast and marinade to a large roasting pan. Pour ½ cup (120 ml) water into the plastic bag and swoosh it around to get as much of the marinade as you can, and pour over the roast. Cover the roast with a lid or foil and cook in the oven until it can be pierced easily with a fork, 3–4 hours.

Remove the roast from the oven and let cool slightly. Transfer the roast to a cutting board and slice it against the grain. Transfer to a serving dish and drizzle the remaining marinade and garlic cloves from the roasting pan over the top of the roast. (If you would like to thicken up the remaining marinade, transfer it to a small pot and cook over medium-high heat for 5 minutes. Allow the sauce to cool slightly before drizzling over the roast. The sauce will continue to thicken as it cools.) Before serving, top the sliced roast with the basil leaves.

MAKE-AHEAD TIP *Tamari garlic beef roast can be marinated for up to 48 hours in the fridge. Cooked and sliced roast should be cooled completely before storing in the fridge for up to 4 days.*

CAN I FREEZE IT? *The roast can be cooked, sliced, and stored in the freezer for up to 2 months. Thaw in the fridge overnight or on the counter for a few hours.*

HOW TO REHEAT *Reheat in a 300°F (150°C) oven until hot, 20 minutes. Add the basil after reheating.*

MAKES 6 SERVINGS

The expression "set it and forget it" was made for this recipe—it's just a few basic ingredients whisked together and smothered over ribs. Slow-cook them over low heat all day in the oven, and when they emerge from the oven, they will be falling off the bone *like butta*. My secret is to place the ribs under the broiler for just a few minutes before serving to crisp up the tops.

ALL-DAY SHORT RIBS WITH GINGER BARBECUE SAUCE

Four 3-bone racks of short ribs

Kosher salt and freshly ground black pepper

1 **tablespoon grated fresh ginger**

1 **cup (240 ml) Homemade BBQ Sauce (page 34)**

Preheat the oven to 250°F (120°C) or set a slow cooker on Low.

Season the ribs on both sides with salt and pepper. Stir the ginger into the barbecue sauce. Place the ribs in a large roasting pan or in the slow cooker and pour the sauce over. Move the ribs around to ensure that they are well coated. Cook, covered, until very tender, 6 hours.

Remove the ribs from the oven and set aside. If transferring to another dish, reserve the cooking liquid. About 15 minutes before serving, turn on your broiler and transfer the ribs to a foil-lined rimmed baking sheet. Brush the tops of the ribs with the reserved cooking liquid. Broil until caramelized, 3 minutes. Remove from the oven and let the ribs rest for a few minutes before serving.

MAKE-AHEAD TIP *Short ribs can be seasoned and marinated in the ginger barbecue sauce and stored in the fridge for up to 48 hours before cooking. Cooked short ribs can be stored in the fridge for up to 4 days.*

CAN I FREEZE IT? *Short ribs can be stored in the freezer for up to 2 months. Thaw in the fridge overnight or on the counter for a few hours.*

HOW TO REHEAT *Reheat in a 300°F (150°C) oven until hot, 20 minutes.*

MAKES 4–6 SERVINGS

A few years ago I traveled to Australia, where my cousin Kelly hosted a big Shabbat dinner. On her buffet table was a gorgeous bowl of pulled lamb, speckled with ruby pomegranate arils and green parsley. Alongside, a huge platter of hummus. I practically stood beside it the entire night! This is my version of very slow-cooked lamb, seasoned with Moroccan spices and simmered in white wine. I'd never refuse a serving of it, no matter the time of day!

PULLED LAMB SHOULDER WITH RED ONIONS, PARSLEY & POMEGRANATE

3 red onions, cut into 8 pieces

1 bone-in lamb shoulder, 3–4 lb (1.4–1.8 kg)

Kosher salt and freshly ground black pepper

2 tablespoons Roasted Garlic Paste (page 29) or 6 cloves garlic, minced

1 teaspoon ground cumin

1 teaspoon ground cinnamon

1 teaspoon dried mint

Juice of 1 lemon

¼ cup (60 ml) extra-virgin olive oil

2 cups (475 ml) white wine

2 cups (475 ml) water

1 bunch fresh flat-leaf parsley, finely chopped

1 cup (160 g) pomegranate seeds

Pomegranate syrup for drizzling

Place the onions in a large roasting pan. Generously season the lamb with salt and pepper, inside and out. Place the lamb over the onions.

In a small bowl, whisk together the garlic, cumin, cinnamon, mint, lemon juice, and oil. Pour this marinade over the lamb and onions, and use your hands to massage in the marinade. Cover and marinate in the fridge for 2 hours and up to 48 hours. Remove from the fridge 1 hour before cooking.

Preheat the oven to 325°F (160°C). Pour the wine and water over the lamb. Cover the lamb and cook in the oven for 4 hours.

After 4 hours, uncover the lamb, and raise the temperature to 450°F (230°C). Roast, uncovered, for 30 minutes. Remove from the oven, cover loosely with aluminum foil, and allow the meat to rest for 20 minutes. Uncover and shred the lamb with a large fork. Stir in the parsley and pomegranate seeds. Before serving, drizzle the top of the shredded lamb with pomegranate syrup.

MAKE-AHEAD TIP *The lamb shoulder can be marinated and stored in the fridge for up to 48 hours in an airtight container or lock-top plastic bag. Cooked and pulled lamb shoulder may be shredded and stored in the fridge for up to 5 days (before mixing in the parsley and pomegranate). The dish can be stored in the fridge for up to 3 days.*

CAN I FREEZE IT? *Pulled lamb shoulder can be stored in the freezer for up to 2 months in an airtight container or a lock-top plastic bag.*

HOW TO REHEAT *Thaw in the fridge overnight. Let the lamb come to room temperature before reheating in a preheated 350°F (180°C) oven for 5–7 minutes.*

MAKES 6–8 SERVINGS

Hamin, also known as *cholent,* is a hearty peasant stew that developed to conform with Jewish laws that prohibit cooking on the Sabbath. The pot is brought to a boil on Friday before the Sabbath begins, then placed in a low oven or a slow-cooker until the following day. Though it is by no means fancy, it is nourishing and comforting, perfect for the long winter months. You may certainly replace the chickpeas with the bean of your choice, or omit completely.

OVERNIGHT CHICKEN HAMIN STEW

2   cups (400 g) dried chickpeas or 2 cans (15 oz/425 g *each*) chickpeas

2   tablespoons canola oil

1   teaspoon cinnamon

3   tablespoons silan (date syrup) or honey

1   whole chicken, cut into 8 pieces and patted dry
    Kosher salt and freshly ground black pepper

6   eggs

4   whole sweet potatoes, washed and peeled

4   whole Yukon Gold potatoes, washed and peeled

If using dried chickpeas, you will need 1 hour to quick-soak them. Put the chickpeas in a large pot and cover with water. The chickpeas will expand to more than double their size, so make sure you cover them by several inches of water to allow for expansion. Bring the chickpeas to a boil and boil for 5 minutes. Remove from the heat and drain. (If using canned chickpeas, simply drain and rinse the chickpeas before adding to the pan.)

Preheat the oven to 350°F (180°C) or set your slow cooker on Low. In a roasting pan or slow cooker, stir together the oil, cinnamon, silan, and chickpeas. Season the chicken pieces on both sides with salt and pepper. Place the chicken pieces on the chickpeas and add the whole (uncracked) eggs and sweet potatoes on top. Fill the pan with water to cover all of the ingredients, filling the pot almost completely to the top.

For Oven Cooking Cover and place in the oven for 1 hour. Reduce the temperature to 250°F (120°C) and cook overnight, for up to 26 hours. Check after 8 hours or so, and refill with water to the top. (You can do this just before the Sabbath, if observing.)

For the Slow Cooker Cover and cook on Low overnight, for up to 26 hours. Check after 8 hours or so, and refill with water to the top. (You can do this just before the Sabbath, if observing.)

To serve, prepare a large serving tray. Remove the eggs, place them in a bowl of cold water until they are cool to the touch, and peel. Use a large slotted spoon to scoop out the chicken and potatoes and place on the tray. Add the chickpeas and peeled eggs. Spoon some sauce over the entire tray. Serve.

MAKE-AHEAD TIP *The stew can be prepared and cooked up to 26 hours in advance.*

HOW TO REHEAT *Keep the stew warm in the oven or slow cooker until ready to serve.*

MAKES 4–6 SERVINGS

It doesn't get stickier, richer, or more tasty than this recipe. Slow-cooked chicken thighs infused with deep-flavored figs, red wine, and a touch of rosemary. The neighbors will come knocking! I often swap the dried figs for fresh figs when they are readily available in the early fall. This dish works really well around Thanksgiving time as the weather gets a little chilly.

STICKY CHICKEN THIGHS IN FIG-WINE SAUCE

10	chicken thighs, skin on and bone in, trimmed of excess skin and fat
¼	cup (60 ml) honey
¼	cup (60 ml) ketchup or tomato paste
¼	cup (60 ml) soy sauce
2	tablespoons olive oil
⅓	cup (75 ml) dry red wine
2	cloves garlic, minced
1	tablespoon dried rosemary
½	cup (80 g) dried Turkish figs, stemmed and halved

Place the chicken thighs in a large roasting pan. Combine the honey, ketchup, soy sauce, olive oil, wine, garlic, rosemary, and figs in a small bowl and pour over the chicken. Cover tightly with foil and marinate in the refrigerator for at least 30 minutes or up to overnight.

Preheat the oven to 350°F (180°C).

Roast the chicken, covered, for 30 minutes. Raise the oven temperature to 400°F (200°C). Uncover and roast until the chicken is crispy on the outside, 20–30 minutes longer.

MAKE-AHEAD TIP *Sticky chicken thighs can be assembled and marinated in the fridge for up to 48 hours. Bring to room temperature before cooking. Cooked chicken thighs can be stored in the fridge for up to 4 days.*

CAN I FREEZE IT? *The chicken thighs can be stored in the freezer for up to 1 month. Thaw in the fridge overnight.*

HOW TO REHEAT *Let the chicken come to room temperature before reheating, uncovered, in a 350°F (180°C) oven for 7–10 minutes.*

MAKES 4–6 SERVINGS

SALADS
& SIDES

This salad screams "summer." And it will be a showpiece at your next outdoor barbecue. The bright pinks, reds, and greens of this dish entice you to eat with your eyes before even opening your mouth. Combining the small watermelon cubes with the crispy radish slices in a simple, light sesame vinaigrette will leave your guests hankering for more. This one is a keeper.

SPINACH, WATERMELON & WATERMELON RADISH SALAD

FOR THE SALAD

- **6** cups (180 g) fresh spinach leaves
- **1** watermelon radish, peeled and sliced (1 cup/about 15 slices)
- **3** red radishes, sliced (½ cup/about 15 slices)
- **1** cup (150 g) diced watermelon (½-inch/12-mm dice), chilled
- **8** fresh mint leaves, roughly chopped

FOR THE VINAIGRETTE

- **1** tablespoon toasted sesame oil
- **2** tablespoons rice vinegar
- **1** teaspoon raw honey
- **1** tablespoon sesame seeds
  Kosher salt and freshly ground black pepper

To make the salad, in a large shallow bowl, use your fingertips to gently mix together the spinach, radishes, watermelon, and mint.

To make the vinaigrette, in a small jar with a lid, shake together the oil, vinegar, honey, and sesame seeds. Season with a good pinch of salt and pepper. Drizzle the vinaigrette over the salad, toss all together, and serve.

MAKE-AHEAD TIP *The watermelon and mint can be prepared and stored in the fridge in separate containers for up to 2 days. The radishes can be prepared in advance and stored for up to 3 weeks. This salad is best when assembled just before serving.*

MAKES 6–8 LARGE SERVINGS

If someone were to ask me what is my favorite food in the entire world, without a doubt in my mind, I would answer "fresh figs." One of the most memorable culinary moments in my life has been plucking a perfectly ripe fig off a gorgeous tree in Israel and savoring it under the golden sun. Whenever figs are in season, I use them in everything that I can. This salad came to be by simply throwing together what I had on hand; oftentimes, my best recipes are born this way. Truffle honey might not be a staple that you just happen to have in your pantry, but I highly recommend you buy a jar; if you don't have any, simply replace it with regular honey.

FRESH FIGS, BABY TOMATOES, RICOTTA & TRUFFLE HONEY

10 ripe, fresh figs, black or green

2 cups (360 g) baby tomatoes, any variety, halved

2 Kirby cucumbers, sliced into thin rounds

10 fresh basil leaves, roughly chopped

3 tablespoons extra-virgin olive oil

2 teaspoons balsamic vinegar
   Kosher salt and freshly ground black pepper

¾ cup (170 g) ricotta
   Truffle honey

Using a paring knife, gently remove the stems from the figs, and halve the figs lengthwise. Scatter the figs on a platter and add the tomatoes, cucumber rounds, and basil. Drizzle with oil and vinegar, and season with salt and pepper to taste. Toss all together. Use a tablespoon to dollop mounds of the ricotta over the top of the platter. Drizzle the ricotta with truffle honey, and serve.

MAKE-AHEAD TIP *The figs, tomatoes, and cucumbers can be prepared up to 8 hours in advance and stored separately in airtight containers in the fridge. Chop the basil, assemble the salad, and drizzle with oil, vinegar, cheese, honey, and seasonings just before serving.*

MAKES 4–6 SERVINGS

Here is a lovely any-occasion salad made with roasted asparagus and zucchini slices, creamy feta cheese, and ruby pomegranate seeds. This salad is practically a meal on its own. But, if you're feeling hungry or want to pair it with something quick and easy, I highly recommend my 4-Ingredient Arctic Char (page 103). I always serve the two recipes side by side. I often make this salad using leftover grilled vegetables. It's what I call "kitchen recycling!"

ARUGULA WITH ROASTED ASPARAGUS, ZUCCHINI, FETA & POMEGRANATE

1   **small bunch asparagus, trimmed**
1   **small zucchini**
1   **tablespoon toasted sesame oil**
    Kosher salt and freshly ground black pepper

FOR THE VINAIGRETTE
1   **clove garlic, minced**
1   **tablespoon honey**
¼   **cup rice vinegar**
½   **cup olive oil**
1   **teaspoon dried basil**
1   **tablespoon za'atar**
    Juice of 1 lemon
6   **cups (300 g) arugula**
¾   **cup (90 g) crumbled feta cheese**
¼   **cup (40 g) pomegranate seeds**

Preheat the oven to 425°F (220°C).

Cut the asparagus into 1-inch (2.5-cm) pieces and place in a bowl. Cut the zucchini into ¼-inch (6-mm) round slices, and add to the bowl. Pour the sesame oil over the asparagus and zucchini and toss to coat. Season with salt and pepper. Spread in a single layer on a rimmed baking sheet and cook for 10 minutes, toss, and cook for 10 minutes longer.

Meanwhile, prepare the vinaigrette. Combine the garlic, honey, vinegar, oil, basil, za'atar, and lemon juice in a jar. Close the jar tightly and shake well until all is combined. Season with salt and pepper.

Remove the veggies from the oven and let them cool for a few minutes. Put the arugula in a large serving bowl. Toss in the vegetables, feta, and pomegranate seeds. Just before serving, spoon the dressing over the salad and toss together.

MAKE-AHEAD TIP *The roasted vegetables can be prepared up to 24 hours in advance and stored in an airtight container in the fridge. Bring the vegetables to room temperature before adding them to the salad. The vinaigrette can be made up to 1 month in advance and stored in the fridge. This salad is best when assembled just before serving.*

MAKES 6–8 LARGE SERVINGS

I love radicchio; it's bitter and crisp and light and beautiful. What can I say? I get poetic when it comes to radicchio! This salad is slightly off the beaten path—cabbage tossed with radicchio, carrots, and toasted almonds. Shredded cabbage, julienned carrots, and toasted sesame marinade are three essentials that I always have stocked in my fridge—so this salad only takes a few minutes for me to toss together.

CABBAGE & RADICCHIO SLAW WITH TOASTED SESAME MARINADE

1   head radicchio

3   packed cups (270 g) shredded cabbage

3   carrots, peeled and julienned (see page 22)

½   cup (60 g) toasted slivered almonds

½   cup (120 ml) Toasted Sesame Marinade (page 33)

Remove and discard the outer leaves of the radicchio. Cut the head in half and remove the core. Using a sharp knife, shred the radicchio into thin strips. Toss the cabbage, radicchio, carrots, and almonds in a large bowl. Just before serving, spoon the marinade over the salad and gently toss all together.

MAKE-AHEAD TIP *The salad can be assembled and stored covered in the fridge for up to 4 hours. Add the marinade just before serving.*

MAKES 6–8 LARGE SERVINGS

The bright and bold heirloom tomatoes in this salad look gorgeous tossed over a mixture of fresh greens. I mix together mizuna (one of my favorite greens) with torn-up basil and mint leaves. A juicy orange cut into segments and then chopped up into bite-size pieces creates a sort of dressing on its own. The combination of mizuna, basil, mint, and citrus is refreshing and creates layers of flavor and dimension—it's not your average salad, though you might want to eat it every day.

HEIRLOOM TOMATO, CITRUS, OLIVE & HERB SALAD

5   cups (250 g) mizuna or wild arugula

1   cup (30 g) fresh basil leaves

½   cup (15 g) fresh mint leaves

4   heirloom tomatoes of your choice, cut into wedges

1   seedless orange

¼   cup (30 g) pitted green olives, halved

3   tablespoons extra-virgin olive oil

2   tablespoons good balsamic vinegar

Kosher salt and freshly ground black pepper

In a large bowl, toss together the mizuna, basil, and mint. Add the tomatoes.

Using a sharp knife, cut a slice off the top and bottom of the orange just far enough to expose the flesh. Place the orange cut side down so that it is sturdy on your cutting board, and cut away the peel. Cut away as much of the peel and white pith as possible by following the orange's shape. Now, holding the fruit in one hand, cut along each side of the membranes that separate the orange segments to free the segments. Cut the orange segments into smaller, bite-size pieces, and add to the salad along with the olives.

Drizzle the oil and balsamic vinegar over the salad, and season with ¼ teaspoon salt and ¼ teaspoon pepper. Use your hands to toss all together. Serve at once.

MAKE-AHEAD TIP *The basil, mint, tomatoes, orange, and olives can be prepared and stored in separate containers in the fridge up to 8 hours in advance. This salad is best when assembled just before serving.*

MAKES 6–8 LARGE SERVINGS

KEEP THE SETUP SIMPLE BY
STACKING YOUR PLATES AND
USING CLEAN WHITE LINEN
NAPKINS. ADD A FEW BUD VASES
FILLED WITH FRESH FLOWERS FOR
A PERSONAL TOUCH. I BOUGHT
THESE BUD VASES AT THE DOLLAR
STORE YEARS AGO, AND THEY
ALWAYS COME IN HANDY! PROOF
THAT YOU DON'T ALWAYS NEED
TO SET A FORMAL TABLE.

This is my go-to lunch on any given day. I love that kale has a more coarse texture than most other greens or lettuces and can stand up to the chopped tomatoes and cucumbers without getting mushy. I'm very particular (maybe even annoyingly so?) about chopping the veggies in this salad exactly the same size. You can do so by using a large chef's knife or a handheld vegetable chopper.

CHOPPED KALE, AVOCADO & ZA'ATAR

1   **bunch green kale, tough stems removed**

1   **large ripe beefsteak tomato**

2   **Kirby cucumbers**

½   **small red onion**

1   **jalapeño chile, stemmed and seeded**

1   **avocado, pitted and peeled**

1   **lemon**

3   **tablespoons chopped fresh cilantro**

3   **tablespoons extra-virgin olive oil**

1   **tablespoon za'atar**

     Kosher salt and freshly ground black pepper

Use a large chef's knife to shred the kale into very thin strips. Place the kale in a large bowl.

Use the same knife to cut the tomato, cucumbers, onion, and jalapeño into tiny dice. Try to keep all of the vegetables the same size. Place all of the vegetables in the bowl with the kale. Toss together using your hands.

Halve and pit the avocado, scoop the flesh from the peel with a large spoon, and cut into the same size tiny dice and add to the bowl. Cut the lemon in half and squeeze the juice of 1 half into the bowl. Use your chef's knife to cut away the yellow peel from the remaining lemon half. Discard the peel, and cut the lemon flesh into the same tiny dice, discarding any seeds you see along the way. Add the diced lemon to the bowl.

Sprinkle the salad with the cilantro, oil, za'atar, ½ teaspoon salt, and ¼ teaspoon pepper. Use your fingertips to gently toss together. Serve at once.

MAKE-AHEAD TIP *The kale can be washed and stored in the fridge for up to 2 weeks. The tomatoes, cucumbers, onion, jalapeño, and lemon may be diced or chopped and stored in separate airtight containers in the fridge for up to 4 hours before serving. Avocado, cilantro, oil, and seasonings should be added just before serving.*

MAKES 4–6 SERVINGS

Celery is often underused. It's true. When it comes to soups and stocks, yes, we use celery. But when it comes to fresh salads? Not so much! This crunchy, mild, fresh vegetable is so versatile—it works well with a mix of flavors. The recipe below is a great way to start. Thinly sliced celery tossed with juicy orange segments, chopped shallots, and walnuts and topped with avocado slices. It's simple, but so good!

CITRUS, CELERY, AVOCADO & WALNUTS

4   **celery ribs and leaves, patted dry**

1   **orange, any variety**

1   **small shallot, peeled and thinly sliced**

¼   **cup (25 g) walnuts, roughly chopped**

1   **jalapeño chile, stemmed and thinly sliced (optional)**

2   **ripe avocados**

    Juice of 1 lemon

    Extra-virgin olive oil

    Kosher salt and freshly ground black pepper

Slice the celery ribs and leaves into thin slices, place in a small bowl, and set aside.

Using a sharp knife, cut a slice off the top and bottom of the orange just far enough to expose the flesh. Place the orange cut side down so that it is sturdy on your cutting board, and cut away the peel. Cut away as much of the peel and white pith as possible by following the orange's shape. Now, holding the fruit in one hand, cut along each side of the membranes that separate the orange segments to free the segments. Place the orange segments and any juice in a small bowl, and set aside.

Arrange the orange segments, celery, and shallot on a large platter. Sprinkle the walnuts and jalapeño slices, if using, on top. Halve and pit the avocados, slice thinly, and scoop the slices from the peel with a large spoon. Arrange the avocado slices on the platter. Squeeze the lemon directly over the avocado. Drizzle the platter with oil, and season generously with salt and pepper.

MAKE-AHEAD TIP *The celery, orange segments, shallots, walnuts, and jalapeño can be prepared and stored in separate airtight containers in the fridge for up to 24 hours before serving. Avocado and dressing should be added just before serving.*

MAKES 4–6 SERVINGS

If you don't already own a kitchen torch, I highly recommend buying one. It's a great tool for caramelizing sugars, roasting marshmallows, or even toasting fresh herbs. The light green fennel, bright yellow beets, and lush pink grapefruit make a stunning combination in this light, flavorful salad.

SHAVED FENNEL & BEET SALAD WITH CARAMELIZED GRAPEFRUIT

2   fennel bulbs, trimmed
     and cored

1   cup (240 g) sliced golden beets

1   handful of fresh cilantro
     leaves, roughly chopped

1   handful of fresh mint leaves,
     roughly chopped

1   large pink grapefruit

¼   cup (50 g) sugar
     Juice of 2 limes

¼   cup (60 ml) extra-virgin
     olive oil

1–2 tablespoons pure maple syrup
     or silan (date syrup)
     Kosher salt and freshly ground
     black pepper

Use a mandolin or a chef's knife to slice the fennel extremely thin. Place the fennel on a large serving platter. Sprinkle the beet slices, cilantro, and mint over the fennel.

Use a vegetable peeler to peel the grapefruit, removing as much peel and pith as possible. Use a sharp knife to cut the grapefruit into thin, round slices, each about ¼ inch (6 mm) thick. Place the grapefruit slices on a foil-lined baking sheet and sprinkle the sugar over each slice. Use a kitchen torch to melt and brown the sugar, being careful not to burn it. Alternatively, you may place the slices under a hot broiler for 15–20 seconds. Add the grapefruit to the platter.

Whisk together the lime juice, oil, and syrup. Season with salt and pepper to taste. Drizzle the dressing over the platter and serve.

MAKE-AHEAD TIP *The beets can be sliced and stored for up to 3 weeks. The fennel, beets, cilantro, and mint may be prepared up to 24 hours in advance and stored in the fridge. The dressing may be prepared up to 1 week in advance and stored in the fridge. This salad is best when assembled just before serving.*

MAKES 6–8 LARGE SERVINGS

I love the look of red kale and red beets. I know that salad isn't really supposed to be sexy—but the colors of this one make it so. I use whole endive leaves, peeled off gently one at a time to maintain their beautiful flower-petal appearance, and toss them with the deep red kale, crimson beets, bright green edamame, and forest green dill.

SEXY RED KALE WITH BEETS & FRESH DILL IN MEYER LEMON VINAIGRETTE

4–6 cups (300–450 g) red kale leaves, washed, dried, and roughly chopped

2 Belgian endives, leaves peeled off whole

1 red beet, peeled and thinly sliced

1 cup (180 g) frozen shelled edamame, thawed and rinsed

1 cup (60 g) roughly chopped fresh dill

Juice of 3 Meyer lemons

½ teaspoon whole mustard seeds

½ teaspoon crushed dried rose petals

1 tablespoon honey

¼ cup (60 ml) extra-virgin olive oil

Splash of balsamic vinegar

Kosher salt and freshly ground black pepper

Combine the kale, endive leaves, beet, edamame, and dill in a large bowl or on a platter. Toss all together.

Pour the lemon juice into a glass jar, add the mustard seeds, dried rose petals, if using, honey, olive oil, vinegar, and salt and pepper to taste. Shake well. Spoon the vinaigrette over the salad just before serving.

MAKE-AHEAD TIP *The beet can be sliced and stored for up to 3 weeks (see page 22). The salad ingredients may be assembled in advance and stored, covered, in the fridge for up to 2 hours. The vinaigrette can be prepared and stored in the fridge for up to 1 week. Dress the salad just before serving.*

MAKES 6–8 LARGE SERVINGS

This is a no-brainer recipe made using leftover veggies from my Quick Vegetable Broth (page 17). It always pains me to throw away all the veggies used to make fragrant broth, so this recipe is my solution. Once the vegetables are completely cooked and softened in the broth, simply mash the onions, potatoes, carrots, and turnips, drizzle with a bold green pesto oil, and enjoy. And, if there are any babies in your house—this mash is the perfect homemade baby food!

AROMATIC VEGGIE MASH WITH PESTO OIL DRIZZLE

FOR THE MASH

- 2 yellow onions, peeled and cooked
- 4 carrots, peeled and cooked
- 1 squash, cooked
- 2 turnips, cooked
- 1–2 potatoes, peeled and cooked
- 1 sweet potato, peeled and cooked

  Kosher salt and freshly ground black pepper

FOR THE PESTO OIL

- ¼ cup (15 g) minced fresh basil or flat-leaf parsley
- 2 tablespoons pine nuts, pounded in a mortar
- 3 cloves garlic, pounded in a mortar
- 2 cups (500 ml) extra-virgin olive oil

To prepare the mash, once the vegetables have been cooked in the broth and are still hot, use a large mesh strainer or skimmer to scoop out the vegetables. Use a potato masher or a potato ricer to mash the onions, carrots, squash, turnips, and potatoes. Place all into a large bowl and mix together. If the mixture is too thick, stir in a few tablespoons of vegetable stock. Season well with salt and pepper. Cover with plastic wrap and keep in a warm spot.

To prepare the pesto oil, in a glass jar or squirt bottle, shake together the basil, pine nuts, garlic, olive oil, ½ teaspoon salt, and ¼ teaspoon pepper.

Use an ice-cream scoop to scoop a mound of veggie mash onto a dish. Drizzle with pesto oil and serve.

MAKE-AHEAD TIP *Vegetables can be cooked, removed from the liquid, and stored in an airtight container for up to 2 days before mashing. Bring them to room temperature before mashing. Aromatic veggie mash can be stored in the fridge for up to 3 days. Pesto oil may be prepared and stored in the pantry for up to 1 week.*

HOW TO REHEAT *Aromatic veggie mash can be reheated, covered, in a 325°F (165°C) oven for 10–15 minutes.*

MAKES 4–6 SERVINGS

These days, it seems as though iceberg lettuce is getting the cold shoulder. I think it's been replaced by mesclun greens and kale. However, I grew up eating crunchy, fresh salads made with iceberg lettuce, and I still love it. This is a delicious salad that is easy to prepare and a major crowd-pleaser. The turmeric and yogurt come together to make a silky, creamy drizzle—a wonderful contrast to the bright, crisp lettuce.

ICEBERG WEDGES WITH RED-ROASTED CHICKPEAS & CREAMY TURMERIC DRIZZLE

1   head iceberg lettuce

FOR THE CREAMY TURMERIC DRESSING

½   cup (125 g) whole-fat plain yogurt
    Juice of 1 lemon

2   tablespoons chopped chives

½   teaspoon Roasted Garlic Paste (page 29) or 1 small clove garlic, minced

¼   teaspoon turmeric
    Kosher salt and freshly ground black pepper

1½ tablespoons extra-virgin olive oil

¾   cup (85 g) Addictive Red-Roasted Chickpeas (page 39)

3   scallions, roughly chopped

To prepare the iceberg wedges, peel a few leaves off the outside of the lettuce head and cut the head in half lengthwise. Cut each half into 3 wedges. Swoosh the wedges around in a bowl of cold water, then let dry on paper towels.

To prepare the creamy turmeric dressing, in a small bowl, whisk together the yogurt, lemon juice, chives, garlic, turmeric, ½ teaspoon salt, and ¼ teaspoon pepper. Stir in the olive oil.

To assemble, place 1 lettuce wedge on a serving plate and drizzle 1 tablespoon of the creamy dressing over the lettuce. Sprinkle 1 tablespoon of Red-Roasted Chickpeas and a pinch of chopped scallions over the tops, and serve.

MAKE-AHEAD TIP *The iceberg lettuce wedges can be prepared, rinsed, and dried up to 3 hours in advance. The iceberg lettuce can be dried on paper towels for up to 1 hour after cleaning and then transferred to an airtight container in the fridge until ready to assemble. (Lettuce should be cold for serving.) The dressing can be prepared and stored in the fridge for up to 3 hours before serving.*

MAKES 6 SERVINGS

Fresh, colorful, crunchy, and delicious—just what a salad should be! The addition of mellow golden raisins and a drizzle of raw tahini add just the right amount of earthiness to this salad. This tahini dressing has become so liked by my family and friends that I've started serving it on my crudité board as well.

CABBAGE SLAW WITH GOLDEN RAISINS & TAHINI DRIZZLE

FOR THE SLAW

- 3 packed cups (270 g) shredded red cabbage
- 3 packed cups (270 g) shredded savoy cabbage
- 3 carrots, peeled and julienned
- ½ red onion, thinly sliced
- ¼ cup (45 g) golden raisins

FOR THE VINAIGRETTE

- ½ cup (120 ml) light olive oil
- ½ cup (120 ml) red wine vinegar
- ¼ cup (60 ml) pure maple syrup
  Juice of 1 orange
- 1 tablespoon whole-grain Dijon mustard
  Kosher salt and freshly ground black pepper
- 2 tablespoons raw tahini for drizzling

To make the slaw, combine the cabbages, carrots, onion, and raisins in a large bowl and toss together.

To make the vinaigrette, combine the oil, vinegar, maple syrup, orange juice, mustard, ¼ teaspoon salt, and ¼ teaspoon pepper in a glass jar with a lid, cover, and shake until combined. Spoon the dressing over the slaw, one spoonful at a time, just until the cabbage is coated—not too much.

Drizzle the tahini over the top of the salad, and serve.

MAKE-AHEAD TIP *The slaw ingredients can be tossed together and stored, covered, in the fridge for up to 8 hours. The vinaigrette can be prepared and stored in the fridge for up to 2 weeks. Dress the salad and drizzle the tahini just before serving.*

MAKES 6–8 LARGE SERVINGS

This might be the simplest and easiest broccoli recipe you've come across. Just a few ingredients and ready in less than ten minutes—my kind of side dish. Broccoli and ginger are a favorite combination of mine. Don't worry about the ginger being too overpowering. When heated, it sweetens up and loses some intensity.

CHARRED BROCCOLI WITH GINGER & SEA SALT

2 tablespoons extra-virgin olive oil

1 large head of broccoli, cut into florets

2 tablespoons minced fresh ginger (you may use jarred minced ginger if you prefer)

Sea salt and freshly ground black pepper

In a grill pan, heat the oil over medium-high heat. Add the broccoli florets and sauté, covered, for 2 minutes. Uncover and char the broccoli until black char marks appear, turning as needed, 5–7 minutes. Add the ginger and sauté, stirring, for 1–2 minutes. Remove from the heat and season with ½ teaspoon salt and ¼ teaspoon pepper. Serve.

MAKE-AHEAD TIP *Charred broccoli with ginger and sea salt is best made just before serving.*

HOW TO REHEAT *Reheat, uncovered, in a 350°F (180°C) oven for 5–10 minutes.*

MAKES 4–6 SERVINGS

Kadaif, also known as kataifi, or shredded filo dough, can be found in well-stocked grocery stores, Greek or Middle Eastern markets, or online. Kadaif is a very useful ingredient to have in your freezer at all times. When baked, the dough crisps up and is melt-in-your-mouth delicious. The key is to keep the thin, angel hair–like dough moistened with butter or oil. In this recipe, sautéed onions, spinach, and edamame are rolled in golden, crispy kadaif and baked in the oven. The result is amazing! If you're looking for a unique side dish, this one is for you.

KADAIF NESTS FILLED WITH SPINACH, CARAMELIZED ONIONS & EDAMAME MASH

½   **cup (120 ml) light-tasting olive oil**

1   **large yellow onion, minced**

1   **box (10 oz/280 g) frozen spinach, thawed and squeezed of excess liquid**

1   **teaspoon ground nutmeg**

1   **cup (180 g) frozen shelled edamame, thawed and rinsed**

    Kosher salt and freshly ground black pepper

    Half of a 16-oz (500-g) box kadaif, thawed

¼   **cup (60 ml) coconut oil, melted**

In a large sauté pan, heat 1 tablespoon of the olive oil over medium-high heat. Add the onion and cook until softened and light brown in color, about 5 minutes. Add the spinach and nutmeg and stir to combine. Cook over medium heat for 5 minutes longer. Remove from the heat and let cool for a few minutes. Transfer to a food processor and add the edamame. Process, using quick on-off pulses, until all ingredients are combined, just a few seconds. Season generously with salt and pepper.

Preheat the oven to 375°F (190°C) and grease a 10-by-12-inch (25-by-30-cm) glass baking dish.

Pull about a golf ball-size piece of the kadaif from the package and spread flat on the counter. Combine the remaining olive oil and the coconut oil in a small bowl and stir together. Brush a little of the oil mixture over the kadaif. Place a heaping tablespoon of the spinach filling onto one end of the kadaif and roll inward into a ball shape. Place in the prepared baking dish. Repeat until you have used all of the filling. Brush a little additional oil over the top of each nest. Cover loosely with aluminum foil and bake until golden and crisp, 20–30 minutes. For slightly darker tops, uncover and bake for a few minutes longer.

MAKE-AHEAD TIP *Spinach, caramelized onion, and edamame mash can be made and stored in an airtight container in the fridge for up to 3 days. Filled kadaif nests can be stored in an airtight container in the fridge for up to 2 days.*

CAN I FREEZE IT? *Filled kadaif nests can be stored in an airtight container in the freezer for up to 1 month. Thaw in the fridge overnight or on the counter for a few hours.*

HOW TO REHEAT *Reheat, uncovered, in a 300°F (150°C) oven for 10 minutes.*

MAKES 6–8 SERVINGS

Has anyone else noticed the amazing array of colors that carrots come in these days? Rainbow carrots, as they are referred to, are a breed of heirloom carrots created from heirloom yellow, purple, and red seeds and are sweeter than regular carrots. The colorful carrots, simply roasted with chickpeas and onions, make a gorgeous and nutritious vegetable side dish. Serve this on its own or with a dollop of my Dill & Lemon Sip (page 32).

ROASTED RAINBOW CARROTS, CHICKPEAS & ONIONS

1   can (15 oz/430 g) chickpeas

10 rainbow carrots, peeled and trimmed

2   yellow onions, peeled and cut into quarters

2   tablespoons extra-virgin olive oil

    Juice of 2 lemons

1   tablespoon paprika

½   teaspoon cumin

    Kosher salt and freshly ground black pepper

3   tablespoons chopped fresh flat-leaf parsley

Preheat the oven to 400°F (200°C). Line a rimmed baking sheet with parchment paper.

Drain the chickpeas and rinse them under cold water. Set out a large, clean dish towel and pour the chickpeas on the towel. Cover the chickpeas with paper towels and gently pat to absorb any excess water.

Once the chickpeas are dry, transfer them to a large bowl. Add the carrots, onions, oil, lemon juice, paprika, and cumin. Toss all together using your hands to ensure that all the ingredients are coated. Season with 1 teaspoon salt and ½ teaspoon pepper and toss again.

Transfer the vegetables and marinade to the prepared baking sheet, spreading them out in an even, single layer. Bake, uncovered, for 40 minutes (if you remember, shake the pan once midway through cooking to ensure even cooking). Sprinkle the chopped parsley over the top, and serve.

MAKE-AHEAD TIP *The rainbow carrots, chickpeas, and onions can be marinated and stored, covered, in the fridge for up to 4 hours before roasting in the oven. Once roasted, they can also be stored in the fridge for up to 3 days.*

HOW TO REHEAT *Reheat, uncovered, in a 300°F (150°C) oven for 10 minutes.*

MAKES 4–6 SERVINGS

This trend began in Israel, where whole roasted cauliflower is a staple in most homes, and it has found its way into kitchens around the world. Not only does it make a stunning and impressive presentation, but this family-style method of preparing and serving everyone's favorite edible flower is also easier than you'd think! By precooking the whole cauliflower with just a little bit of water on the stove top, you are essentially steaming the cauliflower and cooking it through—roasting in the oven then produces a crispy, golden outside while maintaining a soft, buttery inside.

WHOLE ROASTED CAULIFLOWER WITH OLIVE OIL & SEA SALT

1   **whole cauliflower, trimmed of some, but not all, green leaves**

2–3   **tablespoons extra-virgin olive oil**

1   **teaspoon sea salt**

Place the whole cauliflower in a large pot with a tight-fitting lid. Pour 2 cups (500 ml) of water in the pot and cover. Bring to a boil and boil for 13 minutes. Remove the pot from the heat and uncover. Let cool for 10 minutes. Remove the cauliflower from the pot, being careful to keep it whole, and let cool completely on a plate for 10 minutes longer.

Preheat the oven to 425°F (220°C). Line a rimmed baking sheet with parchment paper.

Transfer the cauliflower to the prepared baking sheet. Drizzle the oil over the cauliflower and use your hands to rub the oil all over the top. Sprinkle the salt all over. Bake on the center rack of the oven until golden and crisp, 20–30 minutes.

MAKE-AHEAD TIP *Whole roasted cauliflower can be cooked and kept in a warm oven (200°F/95°C) for up to 2 hours.*

HOW TO REHEAT *Whole roasted cauliflower can be reheated, uncovered, in a 300°F (150°C) oven for 5–10 minutes.*

MAKES 4–6 SERVINGS

To achieve the simple perfection of this recipe, you will need three parchment paper-lined baking sheets. Strewing them scantily with thinly sliced vegetables allows the vegetables to roast in the oven without overcrowding or steaming. In a sense, they almost "air roast"—shriveling and crisping up in the oven, resulting in an earthy and flavorful dish.

ROASTED LEEKS, SQUASH & FANCY MUSHROOMS

1   small butternut squash, peeled and seeded

2   bunches leeks, trimmed

2   cups (460 g) thinly sliced shiitake mushrooms

4   portobello mushrooms, thinly sliced

3   tablespoons extra-virgin olive oil

2   teaspoons herbes de Provence
     Kosher salt and freshly ground black pepper

Preheat the oven to 375°F (190°C). Line 3 rimmed baking sheets with parchment paper.

Use a large chef's knife to cut the squash into thin slices, about ⅛ inch (3 mm) thick. Slice the leeks lengthwise into long strips about ½ inch (12 mm) thick, swish them in a large bowl of water to remove any grit, and pat dry. In a large bowl, toss together the squash slices, leek slices, and the sliced mushrooms. Drizzle with the oil and season with herbes de Provence, ½ teaspoon salt, and ¼ teaspoon pepper.

Transfer the vegetables to the prepared baking sheets, and arrange them in a single layer on each sheet. Do not overcrowd the baking sheets. If necessary, use an additional lined baking sheet. Bake the vegetables in the oven for 20 minutes. Turn the oven off and leave the vegetables in the oven until crisp, 5–10 minutes longer.

Remove the baking sheets from the oven and let cool completely. The vegetables will continue to crisp up as they cool. Peel the vegetables off the parchment paper and place on a serving dish. Serve at room temperature.

MAKE-AHEAD TIP *Roasted leeks, squash, and fancy mushrooms can be baked and stored in an "OFF" oven for up to 8 hours before serving. They can also be stored in the fridge for up to 3 days.*

HOW TO REHEAT *Reheat on a parchment paper-lined rimmed baking sheet in a 350°F (180°C) oven for 5 minutes.*

MAKES 4–6 SERVINGS

I am obsessed with this technique of baking sweet potato halves cut side down on parchment paper. After about an hour in the oven, you will literally peel the sweet potatoes off the parchment paper and be rewarded with a crispy-skinned, caramelized, golden, sticky potato. No mess, no fuss. Thank you to Oz Telem, author of *The Book of the Cauliflower,* for this awesome technique. You can also try it with other root vegetables such as fennel and squash.

CRISPY SWEET POTATO HALVES BAKED ON PARCHMENT

8   **sweet potatoes, scrubbed and dried**

2   **tablespoons light-tasting olive oil**

8   **sprigs of fresh thyme or 1 tablespoon dried thyme**
     Kosher salt

Preheat the oven to 400°F (200°C). Line 1 or 2 rimmed baking sheets with parchment paper.

Cut the sweet potatoes in half lengthwise. Drizzle the oil onto the prepared baking sheet(s). Add the thyme and 2 teaspoons salt and use your fingertips to swirl all together. Rub the potato halves on all sides in the oil mixture and then place the potato halves cut side down on the parchment paper. Bake in the oven, uncovered, for 1 hour. Serve.

MAKE-AHEAD TIP *Crispy sweet potato halves baked on parchment can be baked and left in an "OFF" oven for up to 4 hours.*

HOW TO REHEAT *Reheat, uncovered, in a 350°F (180°C) oven for 10 minutes.*

MAKES 6–8 SERVINGS

Roasted onions as a vegetable side dish? Yes! Versatile onions are often overlooked as a root vegetable to serve solo. Most people think of onions more as an ingredient to add to a recipe, rather than a vegetable to hold its own. That could not be further from the truth! This technique is the same one that I use for my crispy sweet potato halves (facing page). The result? Sweet, luscious, melt-in-your-mouth onion halves. They may surprise your family or guests, but they will also delight them.

CARAMELIZED SWEET ONION HALVES BAKED ON PARCHMENT

6   onions, yellow or red, rinsed and dried

2   tablespoons light-tasting olive oil

8   sprigs of fresh thyme or 1 tablespoon dried thyme
    Kosher salt

Preheat the oven to 400°F (200°C). Line 1 or 2 rimmed baking sheets with parchment paper.

Cut the unpeeled onions in half lengthwise. Drizzle the oil onto the prepared baking sheet(s). Add the thyme and 2 teaspoons salt and use your fingertips to swirl all together. Rub the onion halves on all sides in the oil mixture and then place the onion halves cut side down on the parchment paper. Bake in the oven, uncovered, for 1 hour. Serve.

MAKE-AHEAD TIP *Caramelized sweet onion halves baked on parchment can be baked and left in an "OFF" oven for up to 4 hours.*

HOW TO REHEAT *Reheat, uncovered, in a 350°F (180°C) oven for 10 minutes.*

MAKES 6–8 SERVINGS

Crunchy, lemony, nutty, and green—that's how I would describe these striking vegetables, lightly flavored with citrus and hazelnuts. I like my green beans slightly undercooked so they maintain their crunch and color. Combining the asparagus, broccolini, and green beans is unexpected and satisfying. But the best part is munching on the leftovers the next day.

ASPARAGUS, BROCCOLINI & GREEN BEANS WITH LEMON & HAZELNUTS

6   **Fried Lemon Slices (page 21) or 6 fresh, thin lemon slices, seeds removed**

¼   **cup (40 g) roasted hazelnuts**

2   **tablespoons extra-virgin olive oil**

1   **bunch asparagus, trimmed**

1   **bunch broccolini, trimmed**

1   **lb (500 g) green beans, trimmed**

    Kosher salt and freshly ground black pepper

    Shaved Parmesan cheese (optional)

    Red pepper flakes (optional)

Place the lemon slices and hazelnuts on a large cutting board. Use a large chef's knife to chop the hazelnuts and lemon into tiny pieces. Mix the lemon and hazelnuts together and chop a little more to release their natural oils and juices, then set aside.

In a large sauté pan, heat the oil over medium-high heat. Add the asparagus, broccolini, and green beans. Shake the pan and cover with a lid for 2–3 minutes. This will steam the veggies. Uncover and stir in the lemon and hazelnut mixture. Season with salt and pepper to taste and sauté for 2 minutes longer. Serve topped with shaved Parmesan cheese and red pepper flakes, if using.

MAKE-AHEAD TIP *The lemon slices and hazelnuts can be chopped and stored in an airtight container in the fridge for up to 48 hours. Asparagus, broccolini, and green beans with lemon and hazelnuts can be prepared and stored, uncovered, on the counter for up to 3 hours. They can also be prepared and stored in an airtight container in the fridge for up to 24 hours, but are best served the day made.*

HOW TO REHEAT *Reheat, uncovered, on the stove top over medium-high heat for 5 minutes. Alternatively, reheat, uncovered, in a 300°F (150°C) oven for 10 minutes.*

MAKES 4–6 SERVINGS

Whenever I go out to a Greek restaurant, I order *spanakorizo,* or spinach and rice. I love this dish because it combines the veggie and starch into one delicious, warm, homey dish. This is my version below—it is quick and easy, requiring only a few ingredients that I almost always have stocked at home. I sometimes replace the olive oil with unsalted butter for a richer, more decadent taste.

SPINACH RICE

1   tablespoon light olive oil

1   yellow onion, diced

3   cups (90 g) fresh spinach leaves or 1 box (10 oz/280 g) frozen chopped spinach, thawed and squeezed of excess liquid

½   cup (30 g) roughly chopped fresh dill

1½   cups (300 g) long-grain white rice
     Juice of 1 lemon

½   teaspoon ground nutmeg
     Kosher salt and freshly ground black pepper

2   cups (500 ml) vegetable or chicken broth or water

In a deep sauté pan, heat the oil over medium-high heat. Add the onion and sauté for 5 minutes. Stir in the spinach and dill, and wilt for 2 minutes longer. Add the rice and lemon juice and stir all together. Season with nutmeg, ½ teaspoon salt, and ⅛ teaspoon pepper. Pour over the broth and bring to a boil. Reduce the temperature to low and cover the pan. Cook, covered, until the rice is cooked, about 20 minutes. Serve.

MAKE-AHEAD TIP *Spinach rice can be cooked and stored in the fridge for up to 2 days, but is best on the day it was cooked.*

HOW TO REHEAT *Spinach rice can be reheated, covered, on the stove top over medium heat for 5–10 minutes or in a 325°F (165°C) oven for 10 minutes.*

MAKES 6–8 SERVINGS

Believe it or not, this is one of my kids' favorites! I bathe the kale leaves in white vinegar for just a few minutes before draining, adding olive oil and sea salt, and then baking in the oven. These tangy, crispy chips take just a few minutes to make, hence the 1-2-3, and they're always a hit. They are best when baked just before serving.

1-2-3 SALT & VINEGAR KALE CHIPS

4 handfuls of Washed
   and Stored Kale (page 22)

1 cup (250 ml) white vinegar

2 tablespoons light olive oil
   Sea salt

Preheat the oven to 375°F (190°C). Line a rimmed baking sheet with parchment paper.

Put the kale leaves in a large bowl and pour the vinegar over. Use your hands to push down the kale leaves so they are immersed in the vinegar. Let marinate for a few minutes. Drain, but do not rinse. Transfer the kale to the prepared baking sheet. Drizzle the oil over the kale and season with 1 tablespoon salt. Toss all together using your hands. Bake in the oven until crisp, 15–20 minutes. Transfer to a serving bowl and serve.

MAKES 4–6 SERVINGS

SPECIAL TOKENS CAN REALLY ENHANCE YOUR TABLE. I LOVE USING MY MOROCCAN TEA CUPS AS WINE GLASSES, TO HOLD VOTIVE CANDLES, OR AS BUD VASES.

DESSERTS

Simplicity at its finest. A humble vanilla cake, topped with a mosaic of apple slices, and sprinkled with cinnamon sugar—only this one is made using olive oil, which gives it a rich, Mediterranean taste. Tried and true, this cake will tempt you to make it time and time again.

APPLE & OLIVE OIL CAKE

½ cup (120 ml) light olive oil, plus more for greasing

½ cup (100 g) sugar

2 teaspoons vanilla extract or seeds from 1 vanilla bean

3 large eggs

2 tablespoons milk or almond milk

1¾ cups (200 g) all-purpose flour

2 teaspoons baking powder

½ teaspoon kosher salt

2 apples, peeled, cored and cut into thin slices

1 teaspoon ground cinnamon

1 teaspoon light or dark brown sugar

Preheat the oven to 325°F (160°C). Line the base of a 9-inch (23-cm) springform pan with parchment paper and grease the base and sides with oil.

Using a handheld electric mixer, or a stand mixer fitted with the paddle attachment, beat together the ½ cup (120 ml) oil, sugar, and vanilla. Beat until creamy, about 2 minutes. Add the eggs one at a time, beating each until incorporated. Add the milk and stir on low. Whisk together the flour, baking powder, and salt, add to the wet ingredients, and mix on low until incorporated.

Pour the batter into the prepared pan, and arrange the apple slices on top of the batter, pressing the apples slightly into the batter in any motif you like. Sprinkle the cinnamon and brown sugar over the top of the apples, and bake in the oven until a toothpick inserted in the center of the cake comes out clean, about 45 minutes.

Set the cake on a rack and let cool completely before unmolding and placing on a cake plate to serve.

MAKE-AHEAD TIP *Apple and olive oil cake can be wrapped tightly in plastic wrap and stored in a cool place for up to 2 days.*

CAN I FREEZE IT? *Apple and olive oil cake can be wrapped tightly in plastic wrap and stored in the freezer for up to 2 months. Thaw on the counter for a few hours.*

HOW TO REHEAT *Reheat in a 300°F (150°C) oven for 10 minutes before serving.*

MAKES ONE 9-INCH (23-CM) CAKE

If you've ever thought about baking a carrot cake, but were hesitant, this recipe is the one for you—no mixer needed (except for the icing), you can whip it up in under 5 minutes, and it bakes in less than 30 minutes. I've suggested a traditional cream cheese icing here, but if you'd like to keep it dairy-free, I also love to serve this cake with just a generous sprinkling of confectioners' sugar over the top.

QUICK NO-FAIL CARROT CAKE

⅔ cup (160 ml) canola or rice bran oil, plus more for greasing

1½ cups (175 g) all-purpose flour

1 cup (200 g) sugar

1½ teaspoons baking soda

1 teaspoon baking powder

1 teaspoon ground cinnamon

½ teaspoon ground nutmeg

½ teaspoon ground allspice

½ teaspoon kosher salt

¼ teaspoon ground cloves

3 large eggs, beaten

4 cups (440 g) shredded carrots

½ cup (60 g) chopped toasted walnuts (optional)

CREAM CHEESE FROSTING

½ cup (120 g) cream cheese (block style), softened

¼ cup (4 tablespoons/60 g) unsalted butter, softened

Zest of 1 lemon

Seeds from 1 vanilla bean or 1 teaspoon vanilla extract

3½ cups (350 g) confectioners' sugar

Preheat the oven to 350°F (180°C). Line the base of an 8-inch (20-cm) square or round pan with parchment paper and grease the sides of the pan with oil.

In a large mixing bowl, whisk together the flour, sugar, baking soda, baking powder, cinnamon, nutmeg, allspice, salt, and cloves. In a medium bowl, lightly beat together the ⅔ cup (160 ml) oil and the eggs. Pour the egg mixture into the dry mixture and stir to combine. Fold in the carrots and walnuts, if using. Use a spatula to combine all the ingredients evenly.

Pour the batter into the prepared cake pan. Bake in the oven until a toothpick inserted in the center comes out clean, about 25 minutes. Set the cake on a rack and let cool completely before unmolding and transferring to a cake plate.

Meanwhile, to prepare the cream cheese frosting, use a handheld electric mixer, or a stand mixer fitted with the paddle attachment, to beat together the cream cheese and butter until creamy. Add the lemon zest and vanilla and stir to combine. Pour the confectioners' sugar into the bowl and, with the mixer on low, beat until combined.

Ice the top of the cooled carrot cake with a thick layer of frosting, and serve.

MAKE-AHEAD TIP *Quick no-fail carrot cake can be wrapped tightly in plastic wrap and stored in the fridge for up to 2 days. Bring the cake to room temperature before serving. Cream cheese icing can be stored in an airtight container in the fridge for up to 5 days. The iced carrot cake can be stored in the fridge, covered, for up to 5 days.*

CAN I FREEZE IT? *Carrot cake (without the icing) can be stored in the freezer for up to 1 month. Icing should not be frozen. Thaw on the counter for a few hours before frosting and serving.*

MAKES ONE 8-INCH (20-CM) CAKE

Lemon plus almond? A match made in heaven. This cake is light and humble, but ever so sophisticated and memorable. Served with a glass of mint tea or a scoop of vanilla ice cream, it's a perfect cake for any time of year. I make this cake every year for my husband's birthday.

SIMPLY DIVINE ALMOND CAKE

Canola oil for greasing (spray works well)

1 package (7 oz) almond paste

1 cup (200 g) sugar

1 cup (240 ml) refined coconut oil, in solid form

6 large eggs, at room temperature

1 cup (115 g) all-purpose flour

1½ teaspoons baking powder

¼ teaspoon kosher salt

Zest of 1 lemon

TO GARNISH

Toasted sliced almonds

Fried Lemon Slices (page 21)

Confectioners' sugar

Preheat the oven to 325°F (160°F). Line the base of a 9-inch (23-cm) springform pan with parchment paper. Grease the sides of the pan with a thin layer of canola oil and set aside.

In the workbowl of a food processor fitted with the blade attachment, combine the almond paste and sugar. Add the solid coconut oil and process for 1 minute. Add the eggs one at a time, beating each until incorporated. In a separate bowl, whisk together the flour, baking powder, salt, and lemon zest. Add to the workbowl and process just until all ingredients are combined. Do not overmix.

Pour the batter into the prepared pan and shake the pan to make sure the batter is evenly leveled. Bake in the oven until a toothpick inserted in the center comes out clean, about 1 hour. Place on a rack and let cool completely before unmolding and transferring to a serving dish. Garnish with almonds, fried lemon slices, and confectioners' sugar.

MAKE-AHEAD TIP *Simply divine almond cake can be wrapped in plastic wrap and stored in a cool, dry place for up to 2 days.*

CAN I FREEZE IT? *Simply divine almond cake can be wrapped tightly in plastic wrap and stored in the freezer for up to 1 month. Thaw on the counter for about 1 hour.*

MAKES ONE 9-INCH (23-CM) CAKE

DESSERT DOESN'T NEED TO BE OVER THE TOP BUT IT SHOULD BE MEMORABLE. IT'S ALL ABOUT THE PRESENTATION. EVEN A BEAUTIFUL PLATTER OF FRESH FRUIT ALWAYS SATIATES.

Everyone needs a 5-minute quick-and-easy dish that's a major crowd-pleaser in their menu repertoire. This is it! Even though you're finding this recipe in the dessert chapter, it's really more than a dessert. I serve these gorgeous watermelon slices with wine and cheese, as a summer appetizer, or even as a palate cleanser between courses. You can also prep the watermelon slices ahead and pop them in the freezer to serve them as a frozen treat.

HONEY-DRIZZLED WATERMELON WITH HERBS

1   **small watermelon or ½ large watermelon**

2   **tablespoons honey**

1   **tablespoon chopped fresh basil leaves**

1   **tablespoon chopped fresh mint leaves**

The first step in cutting any round fruit or vegetable is making a flat edge. If you are using a whole watermelon, use a chef's knife to carefully cut the watermelon in half. Place a watermelon half cut side down on the cutting board. For classic wedge pieces, cut the half into slices 1 inch (2.5 cm) thick. Set the slices on a large serving platter. Drizzle with the honey, and sprinkle with the basil and mint. Serve right away.

MAKE-AHEAD TIP *Honey-drizzled watermelon with herbs can be covered loosely with plastic wrap and stored in the fridge for up to 8 hours.*

CAN I FREEZE IT? *Honey-drizzled watermelon with basil and mint can be covered loosely with plastic wrap and stored in the freezer for up to 1 week. Thaw on the counter for 10 minutes before serving (they will still be frozen but slightly softened).*

MAKES 10 SERVINGS

Who doesn't love meringues? They're as whimsical as they are sweet. Simple, crisp, and beautiful on any table. So, why are so many people afraid to make them? I have no idea! They are so easy to make, requiring only a few ingredients, and always a welcome and classic dessert.

MAGICAL MERINGUE KISSES

3   large egg whites, room temperature

½   teaspoon vanilla extract

¼   teaspoon cream of tartar

    Pinch of kosher salt

¾   cup (115 g) sugar

Preheat the oven to 225°F (110°C). Line 2 rimmed baking sheets with parchment paper and set aside.

Place the egg whites in the bowl of a stand mixer or in a clean glass bowl if using a handheld electric mixer. Whisk on medium speed until frothy, about 2 minutes, then add the vanilla, cream of tartar, and salt and mix for 1 minute longer. Raise the speed to high and slowly add the sugar, one spoonful at a time, while whisking on high speed until the mixture is shiny white, creamy, and stiff. This should take about 4 minutes on high speed. You will know the meringue mixture is just right when stiff, pointy peaks are created when the whisk is lifted. (If the mixture is foamy and breaks apart, you may have overwhisked and need to start over again!)

Fill a piping bag fitted with a small tip with the meringue mixture and pipe small rounds, about 1 inch (2.5 cm) wide and 1 inch (2.5 cm) high, onto the prepared baking sheets, spacing them about 1 inch (2.5 cm) apart. If you don't have a piping bag, you can use 2 teaspoons to form small mounds. Bake in the oven for 75 minutes. When the meringues are done, they should be white and glossy and have a little sponginess to them. They will harden as they cool.

MAKE-AHEAD TIP *Magical meringue kisses can be made up to 5 days in advance and stored in an airtight container (I prefer glass because the meringues won't get soggy).*

CAN I FREEZE IT? *Magical meringue kisses can be stored and frozen in an airtight container for up to 1 month. Thaw on the counter for about 20 minutes.*

MAKES 30–40 MINIATURE MERINGUE KISSES

Everyone who has been to my house knows they will always find a big jar of homemade biscotti in my kitchen. Though I tend to stick to the same basic recipe, I sometimes play around with the flavoring to change things up a bit. I came up with this recipe by accident. I combined my husband's favorite flavors (lemon and almond) with my no-fail biscotti recipe. The result is amazing, and now these have become popular among friends and family. I call them "capri biscotti" because these are the flavors of the Italian island of Capri.

CAPRI BISCOTTI

½   cup (100 g) coconut sugar
    or brown sugar
½   cup (120 ml) light olive oil
1   large egg
¼   teaspoon lemon extract
¼   teaspoon almond extract
    Zest of 1 lemon
½   cup (45 g) plus 2 tablespoons
    sliced almonds
1½ cups (175 g) all-purpose flour
½   teaspoon baking soda
½   teaspoon kosher salt

Preheat the oven to 350°F (180°C). Line a rimmed baking sheet with parchment paper.

In a stand mixer fitted with the paddle attachment, beat together the coconut sugar, oil, egg, extracts, and lemon zest on high speed for 1 minute. Reduce the speed to low and add the ½ cup (45 g) sliced almonds, the flour, baking soda, and salt. Beat until a dough forms, about 2 minutes.

Use wet hands to divide the dough into two equal portions. Place the portions on the prepared baking sheet, spacing them about 3 inches (7.5 cm) apart. Shape each portion into a log about 4 inches (10 cm) in diameter and 10 inches (25 cm) long. Sprinkle 1 tablespoon of sliced almonds over the top of each log and use your hands to press the almonds into the top of the logs and flatten them slightly.

Bake the logs in the oven until golden, about 25 minutes. Let cool for 10 minutes on the baking sheet. Reduce the oven temperature to 300°F (150°C). Transfer the logs to a cutting board and use a chef's knife to cut them crosswise into about 15 slices, each about ¾ inch (2 cm) thick. Place the slices cut side down onto the same parchment paper–lined baking sheet, and bake in the oven until the biscotti are crisp, about 10 minutes.

MAKE-AHEAD TIP *Capri biscotti can be stored in an airtight container in a cool, dry place for up to 1 month.*

CAN I FREEZE IT? *Capri biscotti can be stored in an airtight container in the freezer for up to 2 months.*

MAKES ABOUT 30 BISCOTTI

Those who know me know that I am crazy about Nutella. This recipe is the ultimate dessert—chocolatey gooey brownies with chopped hazelnuts and my favorite, Nutella. All in one bowl equals perfection. My kids love these brownies and beg for them every week, though I like to save the recipe for special occasions because they are too addictive. Be forewarned.

ONE-BOWL NUTELLA BROWNIES

½ cup (1 stick/115 g) unsalted butter

1 cup (180 g) semisweet chocolate chips

1 cup (300 g) Nutella hazelnut spread

½ cup (100 g) light or dark brown sugar

2 large eggs

¼ cup (30 g) all-purpose flour

½ teaspoon baking powder

¾ cup (110 g) chopped hazelnuts (optional)

Preheat the oven to 350°F (180°C). Line an 8-inch (20-cm) square pan with parchment paper.

In a small saucepan, melt the butter, chocolate chips, and Nutella over medium heat. Stir until the chocolate and butter are melted and combined. Remove from the heat and transfer to a large bowl. Stir in the brown sugar, eggs, flour, baking powder, and hazelnuts, if using. Stir to combine all the ingredients.

Transfer the batter to the prepared baking dish, and use a spatula to spread into an even layer. Bake in the oven until the center is firm and the top is glistening, 20–25 minutes. Let cool completely before cutting into squares and serving.

MAKE-AHEAD TIP *Brownies can be cut into squares and stored in an airtight container for up to 4 days.*

CAN I FREEZE IT? *Brownies can be cut into squares and stored in an airtight container in the freezer for up to 3 months. Thaw on the counter overnight.*

MAKES 16–20 BROWNIES

This cookie combination includes my three favorite flavors: chocolate, saltiness, and earthiness. These cookies are heavenly! The idea to combine the tahini with just a touch of miso came from a friend of mine, Shushy Turin. I added a mix of milk and dark chocolate chunks into a simple, buttery cookie batter, and the result is indescribable. You really have to taste them for yourself.

TAHINI CHOCOLATE CHUNK COOKIES WITH SEA SALT

- ½ cup (1 stick/115 g) unsalted butter, softened
- ½ cup (120 ml) raw tahini
- 1 tablespoon white miso
- 1 cup (200 g) sugar
- 2 large eggs
- 1 teaspoon vanilla extract
- 1 cup (115 g) plus 2 tablespoons all-purpose flour
- ½ teaspoon baking soda
- ½ teaspoon baking powder
- 1 chocolate bar (3.5 oz/100g) chopped into chunks (I use a combination of milk and dark chocolate)
- 1 teaspoon sea salt flakes

Preheat the oven to 325°F (160°C).

In a stand mixer fitted with the paddle attachment, combine the butter, tahini, miso, and sugar. Beat on high speed until creamy, about 2 minutes. Add the eggs one at a time, beating each until incorporated, then add the vanilla. Add the flour, baking soda, and baking powder and mix on low speed until combined. Stir in the chocolate. Place the batter in the fridge to cool for 10 minutes.

Line 2 baking sheets with parchment paper. Use a small ice-cream scoop to scoop the batter into mounds, placing them about 3 inches (7.5 cm) apart on the baking sheets. Sprinkle the tops with a pinch of sea salt. Bake in the oven until the edges are browned and centers are firm, about 15 minutes. Place on a rack and let cool completely before serving.

MAKE-AHEAD TIP *Tahini chocolate chunk cookies can be stored in an airtight container for up to 4 days. I suggest placing parchment squares between each cookie to prevent sticking.*

CAN I FREEZE IT? *Tahini chocolate chunk cookies can be stored in an airtight container in the freezer for up to 2 months. I suggest placing parchment squares between each cookie. Thaw on the counter for about 20 minutes.*

MAKES ABOUT 16 COOKIES

My kids adore these cookies! They are a cross between a cookie and a brownie and can best be described by the recipe name I've given them. Feel free to swap out the almonds for your favorite nuts. As you'll see, I suggest placing parchment squares (parchment paper that's been cut into small squares) in between each cookie after they have been baked and cooled to prevent them from sticking to one another. This adds another element of fun for the kids—for some reason, mine find it thrilling to peel the cookies off the parchment squares. Go figure.

FLOURLESS CHOCOLATE-ALMOND GOOEY CHEWY GIANT COOKIES

1 cup (90 g) sliced almonds

3 cups (300 g) confectioners' sugar

¾ cup (75 g) almond flour

½ cup (40 g) cocoa powder

2 teaspoons vanilla extract

4 large egg whites, at room temperature

Coarse sea salt for sprinkling

Preheat the oven to 325°F (165°C). Line 2 baking sheets with parchment paper.

In a large bowl, stir together the almonds, sugar, almond flour, and cocoa until well combined. Add the vanilla and egg whites and use a spatula to stir thoroughly until the mixture looks chocolatey and has a firm batter consistency.

Use a medium ice-cream scoop to scoop out the cookies. Place them on the prepared baking sheets 2 inches (5 cm) apart (they will spread while cooking). Sprinkle a few specks of sea salt onto the top of each cookie.

Bake the cookies in the oven until the outsides appear crackly and firm while the insides are still soft to the touch, about 14 minutes. Remove from the oven, place on a rack, and let cool completely, about 20 minutes. Once cooled, peel the cookies away from the parchment paper and place on a serving dish or in a container with parchment squares between each cookie to prevent sticking.

MAKE-AHEAD TIP *The cookies can be stored in an airtight container at room temperature for up to 5 days.*

CAN I FREEZE IT? *The cookies can be frozen (with parchment squares in between each cookie to avoid sticking) but will end up more crunchy rather than gooey. Thaw on the counter for an hour before serving.*

MAKES ABOUT 16 COOKIES

There's nothing quite like a fresh, ripe fig. This recipe uses my favorite fruit, simply dipped in melted chocolate (dark or milk—equally good, the choice is yours) and dusted with crushed pistachios and rose petals. The end result is as gorgeous as it is tasty. These figs are lovely paired with wine and cheese or served on their own when you feel like indulging.

CHOCOLATE-DIPPED FIGS
WITH PISTACHIOS & ROSE PETALS

12   **ripe fresh green or black figs**

1   **bar (3 oz/90 g) dark or milk chocolate, chopped**

3   **tablespoons (20 g) shelled unsalted pistachios, finely chopped**

1   **teaspoon crushed dried rose petals**

    Pinch of sea salt

Line a rimmed baking sheet with parchment paper.

Stem the figs, cut them in half lengthwise, and place them on the prepared baking sheet. In a double boiler or a microwave, melt the chocolate until completely melted. Remove the chocolate from the heat and let cool slightly. Place the pistachios, rose petals, and sea salt in individual small bowls.

Working with one fig half at a time, dip the thicker bottom end of the fig into the melted chocolate and place it back on the parchment paper. Sprinkle pistachios and a touch of sea salt over the chocolate. Repeat with the remaining figs. Place the figs in the fridge until ready to serve.

MAKE-AHEAD TIP *Chocolate-dipped figs with pistachios and rose petals can be stored in the fridge, covered with plastic wrap or in an airtight container, for up to 2 days. Serve directly from the fridge.*

MAKES 12 SERVINGS

INDEX

AT THE END OF THE DAY, THE
TRUTH IS IT'S NOT JUST ABOUT
THE FOOD. IT'S ABOUT THE
MOMENTS AND THE MEMORIES.

KOSHER

WELDON OWEN
President & Publisher Roger Shaw
SVP, Sales & Marketing Amy Kaneko
Associate Publisher Amy Marr
Creative Director Kelly Booth
Art Director Marisa Kwek
Production Designer Howie Severson
Production Director Michelle Duggan
Imaging Manager Don Hill

Photographer Kate Sears
Food Stylist Hadas Smirnoff
Illustrations by Marisa Kwek

Weldon Owen wishes to thank
the following people for their
generous support in producing
this book: Lisa Atwood, Lisa Berman,
Lesley Bruynesteyn, Sarah Putman
Clegg, and Elizabeth Parson.

Produced by Weldon Owen
1045 Sansome Street
San Francisco, CA 94111
www.weldonowen.com

Printed and bound in China

First printed in 2018
0 9 8 7 6 5 4 3 2

Library of Congress Cataloging-
in-Publication data is available.

ISBN 978-1-68188-419-6

ACKNOWLEDGMENTS

THANK YOU:

Amy Marr, Kelly Booth, Marisa Kwek, Amy Kaneko, and the wonderful team at Weldon Owen.

To Kate Sears, Eric Kjensrud, Hadas Smirnoff, and Imogen Kwok for your calm expertise.

To Naomi Freilich, Irene Rofe, Sarah Lasry, Paulina Ashkenazi, Chaya Suri Leitner, Elyse Missry and Eileen Missry, Alexandra Zohn, Elisheva Perlman, and Adeena Sussman—thank you for being a special part of this project.

Andrea Burnett: it's been so many years, and your constant support means so much to me.

Special thanks to Parci Parla Home and Flowers by Victoria for the beautiful dishes, props, and flowers.

I couldn't have done this without my family and friends. For having the patience to answer all of my questions (Gabby, Jessie, Julie, Jeanne, Victoria, and Gabrielle—I know how annoying I was!) and for having the patience to listen to all of my potential book concepts and explanations, thank you for always encouraging me to keep going and cheering me on along the way.

Mom and Dad: I love you and thank you for everything.

Heidi: You were a very big part of this book, from its conception to its realization. I could always count on you for your creativity, positivity, and great advice. You know a lot about a lot. Especially food. Love you.

Jordana: The ultimate *balaboosta*—you've taught me more than you'll ever know. I love you too.

To Jon: This book would not be a reality without you. Thank you for being you, my love.

To Milan, Emanuel, Rafi, and Jude—I'm so proud to be your mom. You guys are my everything. I ♥ you.